D1621797

Cicerone
County Walking Series

WALKING IN OXFORDSHIRE

Wychwood Forest (Walk 10)

WALKING IN OXFORDSHIRE

by
Leslie Tomlinson

CICERONE PRESS
MILNTHORPE, CUMBRIA

© Leslie Tomlinson 1997
ISBN 1 85284 244 X
A catalogue record for this book is available
from the British Library.

Acknowledgements

This book is dedicated to my wife Joan. Without her help and encouragement the work would not have been completed. Together, we enjoyed all the walks and refreshment stops!

I am also most grateful to my daughter-in-law Rebecca for wordprocessing my untidy longhand into a readable manuscript.

Information on The Wilderness, Muswell Hill (Walk 13) was kindly supplied by the National Monuments Record Centre, Swindon.

OTHER BOOKS IN THIS SERIES
Walking in Cornwall
Walking in Cheshire
Walking in Dorset
Walking in Devon
Walking in Durham
Walking in the Isle of Wight
Walking in Kent (2 vols)
Walking in Lancashire

FORTHCOMING
Walking in Northumberland
Walking in Somerset
Walking in Warwickshire
Walking in Sussex

Front Cover: The Thames at Abingdon (Walk 25)

CONTENTS

APPENDIXES

Advice to Readers

Readers are advised that whilst every effort is taken by the author to ensure the accuracy of this guidebook, changes can occur which may affect the contents. It is advisable to check locally on transport, accommodation, shops etc but even rights-of-way can be altered.

The publisher would welcome notes of any such changes.

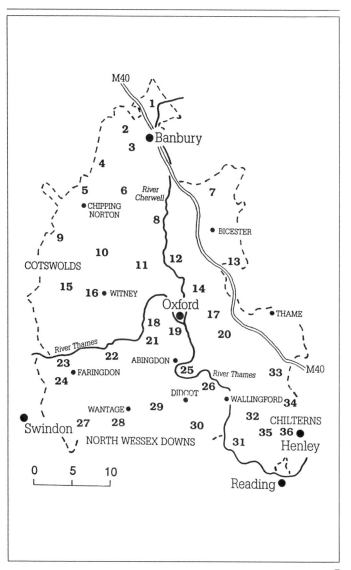

M40

1

2

3 ● Banbury

4

5   6   *River Cherwell*   7

● CHIPPING NORTON

8

9

10   ● BICESTER

COTSWOLDS   11   12   13

15   16 ● WITNEY   14

Oxford

18   17   ● THAME

19   20

21

River Thames   22

23   ABINGDON ●

24   ● FARINGDON   25   *River Thames*   33   M40

26

DIDCOT   ● WALLINGFORD   34

WANTAGE ●   29   ●   32   CHILTERNS

Swindon ●   27   28   30   35   36 ●

NORTH WESSEX DOWNS   31   Henley

0   5   10

Reading ●

INTRODUCTION

The landscape of Oxfordshire is one of remarkable variety. A complex geology, combined with earth movement, erosion and man's handiwork, has created a county of contrasts. Gentle ironstone uplands in the north gradually give way to western Cotswolds hills and a vast central Oxfordshire Plain. Further south, the peaceful Vale of White Horse is bounded by a great chalk ridge - sweeping west to east across the county. The western half of this ridge constitutes the North Wessex Downs while the eastern section, beyond the Goring Gap, forms the Chiltern hills. Although the Cotswolds, North Wessex Downs and Chilterns are Areas of Outstanding Natural Beauty, other regions of the county display equally attractive features.

Largely rural in character, with most of its population concentrated in Oxford, Banbury and a few market towns, Oxfordshire is one huge mosaic of field, hedge and copse, interrupted here and there by the odd village. For the most part, substantial areas of woodland are restricted to Wychwood Forest, Wytham and Bagley woods, and Chiltern beechwoods.

Draining this diverse landscape and adding to its scenic charm are delightful Thames tributaries: Cherwell from the north; Evenlode and Windrush from the Cotswolds; Ock and Thame from the plains. All flow into England's greatest river as it journeys through the county from Buscot in the west, by way of Oxford, to Henley in the east.

With no hills higher than about 850ft (260m) and an absence of steep, lengthy climbs, Oxfordshire is easy walking country. Five long distance paths (**Appendix A**) criss-cross the county. Sections of each are included in the chosen walks. The walks themselves are half-day or easy full-day outings (2 to 10 miles) designed to take in the best of the landscape and to visit places of interest. In many areas there is a choice of two or three routes. The walks can be started from the suggested starting points or from most of the pubs en route. Superb views, picturesque villages, fascinating churches and homely pubs are features of most walks.

My aim has been to provide sufficient detail in the route

descriptions and sketch maps to guide you successfully round each walk. Conventional symbols are generally used on the maps; paths not part of the route are shown as dotted lines and all churches as crosses. Much added pleasure can be gained by having an Ordnance Survey map available to provide further information; O.S. Map numbers are therefore given for each walk.

A car can be stolen or broken into anywhere. To minimise the possibility of it happening to you, police advice is to "choose your parking space carefully. A busy, well-lit area is safest. Thieves don't want to risk being seen." The suggested parking places have been chosen with these thoughts in mind. If you are planning to use a pub, the pub car park is an alternative place to leave your vehicle.

In route descriptions, estimated distances are given in yards; for the present purpose, assume one yard is equal to one metre. Points of interest are shown in capitals - details being provided at the end of each walk.

Most of us walk at an average speed of 2 to 4 miles per hour. If you are not an experienced walker, I suggest a speed of 2 miles per hour be used to calculate the time required for all walks.

To reduce the chance of finding a path blocked by crops or made invisible by ploughing, I have, where possible, selected routes along field edges. If you do encounter blocked paths, please report these to your local group of The Ramblers Association and to Oxfordshire County Council, Countryside Service, Library HQ, Holton, Oxford OX9 1QQ. Thanks to the work of the County Council, other local authorities, The Ramblers Association, and the Oxford Fieldpaths Society, the county's footpath network is gradually improving - but there are still some instances of illegally blocked paths.

At times of high rainfall, paths alongside rivers can also become impassable due to flooding. Vulnerable walks are **Walks 8, 12, 14-16, 18, 21-23, 25, 26** and **31**.

Three walks (**Walks 27, 28** and **30**) traverse Countryside Commission Access Sites. As things stand at present, the public has a right to roam over these sites until September 2001.

Footwear is the walker's most important piece of kit. When conditions are dry underfoot, stout shoes or trainers are adequate; in wet conditions, especially when mud is likely to be encountered, there is no substitute for a good pair of walking boots. In addition, walking socks with double thickness heel and toe regions will help to keep your feet comfortable and problem free.

A recent survey of the diet and health of the British shows that although we have adopted a healthier diet, the number of people dying prematurely from heart disease has not changed. The absence of any improvement is ascribed to a lack of exercise. Walking is one of the easiest ways of correcting this shortcoming. What better way to start walking than by exploring the beautiful Oxfordshire countryside? A combination of gentle exercise, delightful surroundings and amiable companions brings about a mental, spiritual and physical uplift unknown to those who never venture beyond the immediate surrounds of a car park.

On your walks, please follow the Country Code: Guard against all risk of fire; Fasten all gates; Keep dogs under proper control; Avoid damaging fences, hedges and walls; Keep to paths across farmland; Leave no litter; Safeguard water supplies; Protect wildlife, wild plants and trees; Go carefully on country roads - walk on the right-hand side facing oncoming traffic; Respect the life of the countryside.

REFRESHMENTS

Details are provided of selected pubs and tearooms. For pubs, the name of the owner (usually a brewery) is given in brackets. All serve bar meals with food ranging from sandwiches to full three course repasts, depending on the hostelry. Unless otherwise stated, pubs are open for "standard hours". Normally these include the following times: Mon-Sat 12-2pm and 7-11pm, Sun 12-3pm and 7-10.30pm. Establishments on busy roads are often open all day e.g. 11am to 11pm (shown as **11-11**).

Abbreviations used: **SDA** separate dining area; **G** garden or patio with tables; **PA** play area; **CA** children allowed into the dining area and garden, unless otherwise stated; **CM** children's menu; **DA** dogs allowed under control (normally on a lead) inside and outside, unless otherwise stated. Days of the week are shown as: **M, Tu, W, Th, F, Sat** and **Sun**.

Nowadays many pubs and tearooms have carpeted floors. If your boots are muddy, the landlord will not welcome a trail of dirty footprints across his carpet. One solution is to clean off most of the mud with a twig and remove final traces with wet grass or a damp cloth. Alternatively, you can take off your boots and leave them at the door, or put them in a carrier bag and take them inside. Some walkers keep their boots on and tie a carrier bag over each one. Of course, the problem is avoided if you start the walk at a pub or tearoom and arrive by car. Muddy boots can then be exchanged for clean shoes at the appropriate time.

The presence of a village shop is indicated by the letter **S**. Some shops are open six or even seven days a week.

PUBLIC TRANSPORT

For purposes of public transport the County Council has divided Oxfordshire into twelve areas and published a Summary Timetable for each. Free copies of these timetables are available from tourist information offices, public libraries and Oxfordshire County Council, Environmental Services, Speedwell House, Speedwell Street, Oxford OX1 1NE.

Unless otherwise stated, public transport takes you to the start of each walk. The name of the bus or railway company is indicated by one or more capital letters in brackets. The route number is also given for bus companies. The companies are listed in **Appendix B**. Days of the week are abbreviated as for places of refreshment.

Where a walk is served by more than one route, only the two or three providing the most frequent services are listed. Further details of routes and times can be obtained from the Summary Timetables, company timetables or by telephoning the appropriate operator (**Appendix B**).

GEOLOGY

Sedimentary rocks underlying the Oxfordshire landscape were laid down when south-east England was submerged beneath the sea during Jurassic and Cretaceous periods (195-135 and 135-65 million years ago, respectively). During those vast aeons of time, sedimentation falling onto the seabed became layers of limestone, chalk and clay. Later earth movements raised the land above sea level and tilted it towards the south-east.

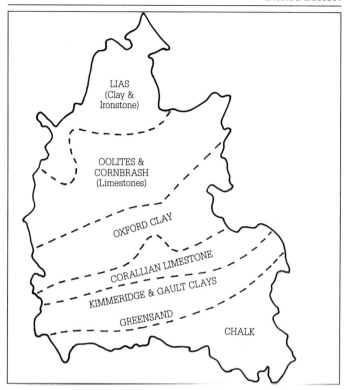

Millions of years of subsequent erosion have resulted in each layer outcropping at the surface. These appear on the map as diagonal bands running south-west to north-east across the county. Eroding more slowly than soft clays, harder limestones and chalk became the hills of Oxfordshire, their steep, north-west scarp faces contrasting with gentle dip-slopes to the south-east. In crossing the county from north to south, outcropping layers thus become progressively younger, with Jurassic giving way to Cretaceous in the Vale of White Horse.

Later geological periods had minimal effect on the county. Remnants of clay and sand deposited about 50 million years ago, when Oxfordshire was once again beneath the sea, are found in small areas of the Chilterns and Downs. In more recent times, glaciation and meandering rivers have created shallow beds of sand and gravel. These cover many of the "outcropping" strata in river valleys.

What has been the influence of geology on local landscapes, building materials and land use? The remainder of this section attempts to give brief answers to these questions, starting in the north of the county.

Beneath the north Oxfordshire uplands is a limestone of high iron content known as ironstone or, more correctly, Marlstone. Rich brown in colour, its widespread use in buildings imparts a feeling of warmth to the local villages (explored in **Walks 1-4 and 6**). Quarries in the region of Hornton are famous for this splendid stone. Around Banbury, the level of iron reaches 28% - sufficient for the material to be mined as iron ore - an industry which continued until the 1950s.

Oolitic limestones form the Cotswolds hills around Burford (**Walk 15**). They also underlie the uplands of Wychwood (**Walk 10**), Blenheim (**Walk 11**) and Juniper Hill (**Walk 7**). For centuries, Great Oolite (Cotswold Stone) - a fine building stone - was quarried in the Burford area. In Stonesfield (near to Charlbury, **Walk 10**), frost action splits the limestone into "slates" - a product which covers thousands of roofs in Oxfordshire and beyond.

Further south, Oxford Clay of the upper Thames valley extends beyond Oxford to the wilderness of Otmoor. This is a flat country of water meadow and willow (**Walks 14, 21, 23**).

Running along the south bank of the Thames from the county boundary through Coleshill, Buckland, Appleton, the Oxford Heights, Beckley and Muswell Hill is a low Corallian ridge. The limestone here contains the fossilised remains of a Jurassic coral reef (hence the name), grown beneath a warm shallow sea. In places, the ridge is capped by clay and/or Greensand (**Walks 13, 14, 17-19, 21, 22, 24**).

Between the Corallian ridge and the great chalk ridge of the Downs and Chilterns lies the clay plain of the rivers Ock, Thame and Thames, which includes the Vale of White Horse. Farmland here is arable, meadow or pasture, with sand and gravel extraction being a major industry of the river valleys (**Walks 25, 26**).

An impervious layer of Greensand/Gault Clay beneath the porous chalk ridge is responsible for springs found at the feet of the Downs and Chilterns. These in turn have given rise to a line of "spring-line" villages, some of which are visited on **Walks 28-30**.

The chalk itself, several hundred feet thick, is made up of the skeletons of microscopic sea creatures. Within the chalk are irregular nodules of silica in the form of flint. In some places, a process of natural hardening has converted deposits of sand into boulders of sandstone. Known as sarsen stones, these are found lying on the surface. As elsewhere, local building materials reflect the local geology, with brick, flint, chalk block and sarsen finding their various uses (**Walks 27, 28, 30, 32-36**).

NATURAL HISTORY

Most of the present-day flora and fauna of Oxfordshire reached the county from continental Europe between the end of the last Ice Age (about 9,000 BC) and 5,500 BC, when a rising sea level turned Britain into an island. Since those times, the steady growth in human population has had an ever increasing impact on the natural environment. In spite of this, the county has a remarkable diversity of wildlife, with over one hundred species of birds breeding here. Plants and animals have adapted to a situation where about 80% of the land is devoted to agriculture, 6% to woodland, 1% is open water/mineral extraction and 13% urban.

In agricultural areas, modern farming methods tend to reduce the range of wild plants and their dependent animals. Contrary to this general tendency, centuries of sheep grazing on the chalk and limestone grasslands of the Chilterns, Downs and Cotswolds have allowed a rich variety of wild flowers to flourish. Calciphile (calcium-loving) plants, tolerant of the dry, alkaline soil include: vetches, legumes, salad burnet, bird's foot trefoil and members of the exotic orchid family, such as the rare monkey, military and ghost orchids. Certain butterflies, e.g. the chalk-hill blue and Adonis blue, live almost exclusively on this type of upland, their larvae feeding on the horseshoe vetch.

Woodland, an important feature of the landscape, is also an important refuge for wildlife. About half of the wooded areas in

Oxfordshire are broad-leaved, the remainder being coniferous or mixed. Oak is the most common of the broad-leaved varieties, except in the Chilterns, where beech dominates. Other species include: sycamore, ash, hornbeam, maple, birch and hazel.

Only those plants tolerant of deep shade in summer and early autumn can thrive under woodland conditions. Of these, the earliest to flower is the snowdrop, which can be seen, for example, on **Walk 33**. Ten walks (**Walks 9, 10, 17, 21, 24, 32-36**) feature another woodland plant - the bluebell; these walks are especially enjoyable when the forest floor becomes a mass of blue in late spring. Other flora adding colour to woodland walks include: wood anemone, primrose, yellow archangel and goldilocks buttercup.

Birds not found elsewhere in the county are attracted to the 0.5% covered by water. Mute swans, mallards, coots, moorhens, Canada geese, grey herons and great crested grebes live on the Thames and its tributaries (**Walks 8, 12, 14-16, 18, 21-23, 25, 26, 31**). A rare sight, and one of the thrills of riverside walking, is the flash of cobalt blue as a kingfisher skims its way across the water's surface. In wintertime, static water such as lakes often features huge flocks of gulls, teal, pochard, goosander, wigeon, goldeneye and tufted duck. An interesting sight for an inland county is a group of cormorants which have taken up residence at Farmoor Reservoir (**Walk 18**). Undoubtedly the local trout are a great attraction.

Bones found in Thames valley gravel beds show that mammoth, hyena, bison, wolf, cave lion and other animals roamed over the county during inter-glacial periods, 70,000-200,000 years ago. Nowadays, badgers and foxes are probably the most numerous of the larger mammals. The former, being nocturnal, is rarely seen while the latter, a shy creature, is only encountered in quiet locations. Roe and fallow deer inhabit forests, parks and nature reserves - such as Wychwood, Stonor and Warburg (**Walks 10 and 34**) - while the tiny muntjac wanders widely across the county.

HISTORY

Man first made an impact on the Oxfordshire landscape during the Neolithic period (3,000-1,800 BC). It was Neolithic farmers - immigrants from the Mediterranean - who first felled trees to create open land for crops and livestock, and introduced the art of pottery.

One of their tracks, the Icknield Way - running east-west across the county - linked centres of population in Norfolk and Wiltshire. It continues in use to this day (**Walks 29** and **33**). Long barrows - those oblong communal burial chambers built of large stone slabs - are undoubtedly the most important monuments of Neolithic man. Fine examples can be seen at Waylands Smithy (**Walk 27**) and the Whispering Knights (**Walk 5**).

Arriving from Europe, new invaders during the Bronze Age (1,800-550 BC) brought with them the technology of metals. They also imported their custom of individual burial in small, round chambers - some of which are passed near to the Ridgeway on **Walk 30**. Recent dating of the Uffington White Horse and adjacent hill-fort as late Bronze Age (**Walk 27**) shows that circular forts of this type, usually associated with the Iron Age (550 BC - 43 AD) were being built about 1,000 BC. Hill-forts believed to be of genuine Iron Age origin are visited on **Walks 24, 26-28**. The largest settlement of this period in Oxfordshire probably flourished on the 114-acre site at Dyke Hills, Dorchester (**Walk 26**).

The Romans settled extensively throughout the county. Dorchester continued as a walled town and of the other settlements only Alchester (near Bicester) had similar status. A north-south road (**Walk 14**) connected the two towns while Akeman Street ran east-west through Alchester, Blenheim Park (**Walk 11**) and Asthall (**Walk 15**).

Being on the border of Wessex and Mercia, Oxfordshire suffered in territorial disputes between the two kingdoms during the early Anglo-Saxon period. Later in the same era, Alfred halted Danish incursions at the battle of Ashdown (871) - somewhere on the Downs, possibly near to Ashdown House (**Walk 27**).

The last successful invaders, the Normans, established baronial estates across the country, some of which remain today. Great hunting forests similar to Wychwood provided sport for kings and any poacher caught within their bounds suffered severe penalties (**Walks 9** and **10**). Houses built at the time in Appleton and Sutton Courtenay are passed during **Walks 21** and **25**.

Vast open fields and large areas of forest covered lowland areas of Oxfordshire during the late Middle Ages, while flocks of sheep grazed the Cotswolds and Downs - bringing great wealth to landowners. Arrival of the Black Death in 1349 heralded a change of fortune as half of the population perished. Some villages, e.g. Tusmore (**Walk 7**), were completely wiped out.

Oxfordshire played a central role during the Civil War. Oxford became the Royalist headquarters and Broughton Castle (**Walk 3**) a secret venue for leading Parliamentarians. The first major encounter took place in 1642 at Edgehill on the Oxfordshire-Warwickshire border, 2 miles north-west of Hornton (**Walk 2**). The battle to control Cropedy Bridge - the most important conflict within the county - occurred three years later. **Walk 1** explores the battlefield.

Enclosure of open fields and heaths in the 18th century resulted in the pattern of small rectangular fields, hedges and copses which cover the county today. In the same century, landscape gardeners Capability Brown and William Kent created another outstanding feature - the great country parks such as Blenheim (**Walk 11**), Shotover (**Walk 17**) and Rousham (**Walk 8**).

From the year 634, when Bishop Birinus first preached at Churn Knob (**Walk 30**), Christianity started to make a lasting impact on Oxfordshire. In the following year he baptised King Cynegils of Wessex and founded a cathedral at Dorchester (**Walk 26**). As the new religion spread, churches were built and abbeys established, e.g. Abingdon Abbey in 675 (**Walk 25**). After the Conquest, stone buildings replaced wooden ones. Many Oxfordshire churches retain architectural features from their Norman ancestry, and a few, e.g. at Checkendon (**Walk 35**), are largely unaltered from those times. The county has a particularly rich heritage of churches. Each one is a unique historical, architectural, artistic and spiritual treasure house. As visitors, we can help to preserve these places for future generations to enjoy.

WALK 1

Cropedy - Oxford Canal

(3¹/₂ miles)

Just over 350 years ago the most important Civil War battle in Oxfordshire was fought at Cropedy Bridge on the River Cherwell. This walk takes us from the picturesque village of Cropedy, across the battlefield, to the Royalist high ground at Williamscot and back along the Oxford Canal. Extensive views over the Cherwell valley and pastoral scenes by the waterside are attractive features of the walk.

O.S. Maps:	Landranger 151. Pathfinder 1022.
Start (467,466):	Park and start at The Green, Cropedy. 4 miles N of Banbury on a minor road off the A423.
Terrain:	Mostly level with an easy hill climb. Two stiles.
Refreshments:	Cropedy: Red Lion (Courage) 01295-750224, SDA, G, CA, CM, DA in G, DA inside in winter. Old Coal Wharf Cafe, W-F 12-5; Sat, Sun, Bank Hols 11-6. S.
Public Transport:	From Banbury: 4(G) Th, Sat; 54(CV), 509(M), 510(M, J) M-Sat.

Route:

1.   When surveyed, none of the footpaths or bridleways used in the walk was waymarked. From The Green walk into CROPEDY village. Go past a craft shop to the beginning of the High Street and turn right down Church Lane. At the end, veer right between bollards. Proceed through a housing estate to reach a T-junction. Turn left. Cross bridges over the Oxford Canal and River Cherwell. There are two inscriptions on the river bridge: one tells of the Civil War battle which took place here in 1644; the other provides historical details about the structure. From the shaded roadside verge, it is difficult to imagine thousands of Roundheads and Cavaliers engaged in furious combat in the fields on your left -

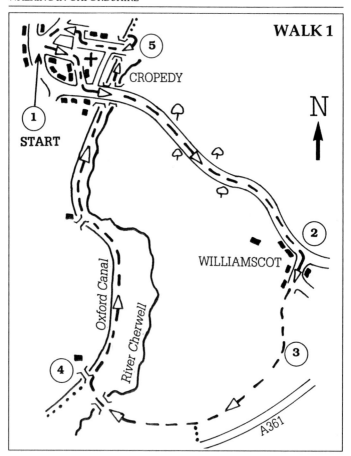

where the battle to control the bridge took place. For the next mile or so our route gently climbs a quiet, dappled road to the hamlet of Williamscot. On the way, the tower of Wardington church can be seen peeping above the left forward horizon.

2. On reaching the hamlet, pass the entrance to Williamscot House and charming ironstone cottages. Charles I spent the night

after the conflict in this hamlet. Swing right down a narrow lane signposted as a cul-de-sac. At Corner Cottage, where the lane curves left, proceed ahead past a white metal barrier and along a farm track for 40 yards to a locked gate. Cross a stile beside the gate. Keep on the track for another 30 yards to reach a second gate. Go through, turn half left and continue to a third gate. Beyond this, our path keeps next to a fence as it dips and ascends to the left-hand corner of a field. You are now close to the summit of Williamscot Hill - where the Royalist rearguard was located prior to the outbreak of hostilities. Enjoy superb views across the Cherwell valley, with Banbury to the left and the village of Great Bourton to your right. It was from Great Bourton that Waller's Parliamentary Army launched its two-pronged attack on the Royalist forces.

3.   Do not go through a gate in the hedge but swing right and descend along the field boundary. Look right for a glimpse of Cropedy - mostly hidden by trees. Pass through a gate in the field corner and proceed ahead on a track running parallel to the left-hand hedge (and A361). When the track swings left, continue forwards to a gate in the far fence. Beyond the fence, a well-used path keeps going in the same direction, gradually curving right towards a gated bridge over the Cherwell. Waller's cavalry forded the river here on their way to attack the Royalist rearguard. On the far bank, veer a quarter right and walk to a red brick bridge over the OXFORD CANAL. Do not cross, but climb a stile onto the towpath. Turn right.

4.   There is time to appreciate the canal-side scenery and slower pace of life as you stroll along the towpath for the next 1¼ miles back to Cropedy. At the outskirts of the village, pass under the first bridge and continue for 200 yards to a second. Picturesque Cropedy Lock and lock-keeper's cottage are just beyond the second bridge. Turn sharply right here onto a road.

5.   Bear right over the bridge and up Red Lion Street. At the top end, a diversion can be made to visit the church. Otherwise, follow Red Lion Street round to the right. In 100 yards turn left. Go past the post office and Methodist chapel to reach the High Street. Swing left and soon arrive back at The Green.

Points of Interest

CROPEDY The village probably grew up as a collection of thatched cottages on high ground next to a ford across the Cherwell. In 1314 the ford was supplemented by a bridge - a structure rebuilt many times since. Although the village has grown with time, the older ironstone cottages retain their ancient charm.

On 29th June 1644 the battle to control Cropedy Bridge took place in fields east of the river. Sir William Waller's Parliamentary Army of 9,500 troops fought a bloody battle here against a Royalist force of 8,500 men, with lesser engagements at Williamscot and Hay's Bridge. Although Waller held the bridge, he lost his artillery and 700 men were killed, taken prisoner or deserted. Royalist losses were light.

The church of St Mary, mostly built during the 14th and 15th centuries, holds an interesting reminder of the Civil War. A rare 15th-century brass eagle lectern, hidden in the river to prevent its destruction during the war, was recovered some 30 years later. It was tarnished to a bronze colour and missing one of its lion feet. A new bronze foot was fitted. Repolishing revealed the mistake, still visible today, with the darker bronze showing up against the brass.

OXFORD CANAL The Oxford Canal is part of the first waterway built to join the coalfields and industry of the Midlands to Oxford and London (via the Thames). James Brindley surveyed and planned the route, but unfortunately died in 1772 before construction was completed. Work started at Coventry in 1769. Twenty-one years later, in 1790, the first commercial traffic moved along the waterway. At first, the canal was successful, conveying coal, grain, stone, bricks and other heavy goods. Cheap coal from the Midlands proved of great benefit to people and industry along the route. However, competition from the Grand Union Canal and railways during the 19th century reduced its viability. Even so, commercial operations continued until the 1950s. Nowadays the tranquil canal is a favourite leisure venue for boating enthusiasts, fishermen and walkers (**Appendix A**).

WALK 2

Wroxton - Shenington

(9¹/₂ miles)

The landscape of north Oxfordshire with its gently rolling hills is little known outside the area. An underlying layer of ironstone gives the soil and buildings a distinctive reddish-brown appearance. Starting from scenic Wroxton our walk explores this attractive countryside, passing through a string of charming villages: Horley, Hornton, Shenington, Alkerton and Balscote. Each village (except Alkerton) has its own pub - so there is no problem about refreshments!

O.S. Maps:	Landranger 151. Pathfinder 1022, 1021.
Start (414,418):	Park and start at the duck pond, Wroxton. 2¹/₂ miles W of Banbury on the A422.
Terrain:	Gently undulating. Twenty-six stiles.
Refreshments:	Wroxton: North Arms (Morrells) 01295-730318 SDA, G, CA, DA in G. Hornton: Dun Cow (Free House) 01295-670524 SDA, G, CA, PA across the road, DA, closed Th lunchtime. Shenington: The Bell (Free House) 01295-670274 SDA, CA, CM, DA.
Public Transport:	From Banbury to the villages: 53(CV) Tu; 511(J), 502/504(M) M, Th, Sat; 270/X70(M) M-F. Allow two days to do this walk by bus.

Route:

1.   For most of the way, our route follows an Oxfordshire Circular Walk, so look out for the appropriate waymarks. It also includes a section of the d'Arcy Dalton Way (**Appendix A**). From WROXTON duck pond walk past the College gates along Church Street. At the end veer left beside the church to reach a road junction. Turn right here onto a signposted footpath ("Horley 2¹/₂"). The path follows a fence and crosses an open field to a line of trees. Go through a gate in the trees. Turn left onto a farm track and in 120 yards cross the A422.

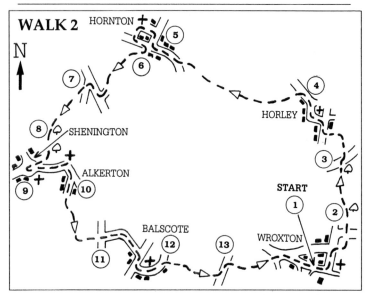

2. Our route does not follow the direction of a bent sign but goes straight ahead over an arable field towards the left-hand edge of a group of trees (Lord's Spinney). Go through the end of the spinney, bear slightly left and walk uphill towards the horizon. Pass through a gap in the next hedge. Turn a quarter right and continue across an open field. Enjoy superb panoramic views, with the village of Horley visible ahead. Aim for a point where the left-hand end of a small wood meets a hedge. Ten yards short of the hedge, turn right into the trees. After a further 10 yards, swing left and cross a stile into a road. Turn right. Follow a downward gradient for 150 yards to a bend in the road.

3. Turn left here under a vehicle barrier onto a disused railway track. The railway was originally built to transport ironstone from local quarries to the main line at Banbury. It operated until the 1950s. In 100 yards bear right over a stile into a pasture. Turn three-quarters left and take a well-worn path to a double stile in the far fence. Beyond the stile our route swings left; it then follows a fence / hedge to the end of a field. Climb a stile here into a road. Turn right

Wroxton guide post

and walk uphill into the village of HORLEY. Fifty yards before a main road junction (next to the Red Lion), turn left into a narrow lane. Soon arrive at the Manor House with its Late Georgian front, opposite entrance gates to Bramhill Manor. The lane subsequently veers right, passes a church and comes to a road junction. Turn left here. In 200 yards bear left between the last two houses onto a farm track leading to Bramhill Park Farm.

4.   This undulating track continues for $1/2$ mile to a gate. Beyond the gate go forwards onto a path gradually ascending to the end of a long, uncultivated field. At the distant hedge, cross a double stile into a pasture. Turn left and climb to the field corner. Turn right, walk to the next corner and turn right again. At the following corner bear three-quarters left onto a track across the pasture to a double stile in the far hedge. Go ahead on a footpath running along the right-hand boundary of the next field. After 150 yards turn a quarter left at a waymarked post and walk uphill to the field corner. Cross a stile into a road. Swing right and descend into the ironstone village

of HORNTON - delightfully situated in a secluded, wooded valley.

5.   At The Green you can take a short walk around the village centre or continue on the main route by turning left onto a Circular Walk path. The village walk bears right for 100 yards and then left down Church Lane to reach the church (open). Leave by a gate at the far side of the churchyard. Follow a lane to a T-junction and turn left. Walk past the Dun Cow. At The Green turn right onto the Circular Walk path leading uphill.

6.   Near to the top of the incline, look right over a gate for a good view of Hornton. For the next mile a fenced bridleway takes us between arable fields and past the buildings of Hornton Grounds farm. Extensive views are to be had from this track. Seventy yards before reaching the A422, turn left along a road leading to Hornton Grounds Quarry. Turn right at a T-junction. In a further 200 yards swing sharply left onto a road signposted: "Recycling and Waste Centre".

7.   After 150 yards, bear right over a stile into a pasture. Veer half left and aim for the far left-hand corner. Look for a stile hidden in a hedge 100 yards short of the corner. Cross into the next field, turn half right and walk to a stile visible in the right-hand hedge. Go over two stiles and a farm track to reach an arable field. Bear half left, aiming for the distant left-hand corner. Enjoy a good view of Shenlow Hill (746ft, 227m) on the right horizon. Gliders can often be seen landing at Shenington airfield in the shadow of the hill. Cross a stile 100 yards right of the field corner and pass through a row of trees.

8.   Our route continues in the same direction through a gate in the left-hand hedge of the next field. It then bears left along a farm track for $^1/_4$ mile to a second gate. Beyond the gate, keep to the track for a further 100 yards before turning a quarter right across rough pasture to the far corner. Cross three more stiles and a stream. Enter a field, turn a quarter right and climb to the top right-hand corner. In 30 yards arrive at a metalled road in the village of SHENINGTON. Turn right. Soon pass the church (open) and come to an extensive village green, with the Bell Inn on your right.

9.   A circular walk will allow you to appreciate the wide variety of buildings encircling this fine open space. When exploration is

complete, retrace your steps down the road. Go past the church and across the valley to ALKERTON. Where the road swings right, climb a flight of steps on the left to reach an unusual church and impressive Jacobean rectory. Leave by a drive alongside the rectory. Cross the road and walk down Well Lane - an idyllic backwater lined with beautiful cottages.

10.   In 150 yards, where the metalled lane veers right, go forwards on a gravelled drive signposted: "Shutford 2". The drive passes between houses and soon becomes a broad grassy track. Descend along the track to a wooden gate. Do not go through, but turn right and then left. In 100 yards pass through a second gate. Proceed ahead for 80 yards across a landscaped garden to a third gate. Beyond this, continue forwards over a pasture and along a track on the right-hand side of a line of hawthorn trees (next to a wooden electricity pole). When the track veers left through a gap in the trees, do not follow it but turn right. Descend along the field boundary to a stile, 50 yards short of the corner. Look back for a good view of Shenington church. After the stile, our path continues along the right-hand side of three fields. At the end of the third field, cross a stile, 70 yards left of the field corner. Immediately swing left through a metal gate and ascend a farm track to reach a road junction. Look back from this track for a last view of Shenington.

11.   Cross the junction and go forwards on a road to Balscote. At a bend in the road notice that the fields on your left lie 10-20ft (3-6m) below road level. These, and many others in the area, have been quarried for ironstone and then restored to agricultural use. In ¹/₂ mile arrive at the village of Balscote (or Balscott). Turn right. Pass the 14th century church, topped with a narrow tower. At a road junction next to the Butchers Arms our route swings left and follows a descending gradient between charming cottages to reach the village green. Continue on the road to the end of the green.

12.   Turn right here onto a waymarked concrete drive climbing to Round Hill House and Manor Farm Office. Beyond the buildings, a fenced farm track takes us for ¹/₂ mile to a T-junction with a road. Turn left.

13.   After 200 yards bear right through a gate and go forwards along a left-hand field boundary. The path passes under high-voltage

electricity cables before coming to the field corner - a $^1/_4$ mile distant. At this point the side of an old quarry reveals the layers of ironstone which extend for about 20ft (6m) below the surrounding fields. Turn left. Walk downhill for 25 yards and then bear half right. Follow a track across an open field. (If the route is not visible, aim for a cottage with three chimneys.) Climb a stile on the far side to reach a road beside the unique Wroxton guide post. Apart from the inscription: "First given by Mr Fran(cis) White in the year 1686", its origin is unknown. Turn left for a few yards and then right along the A422 towards Banbury. In 150 yards swing right into Wroxton. Proceed downhill back to the duck pond.

Points of Interest

WROXTON A picture postcard village of thatched ironstone cottages radiating outwards from a central duck pond. The wrought iron entrance gates to Wroxton College (originally Wroxton Abbey) are nearby. Allow yourself plenty of time to explore the village and extensive landscaped gardens of the college (**Appendix C**). The building has seen many additions since the original structure was erected by Sir William Pope in the 17th century on the site of an earlier priory. It remained in the Pope-North family for over 300 years. During the reign of George III, Frederick Lord North was the Prime Minister responsible for the loss of our American colonies. It is ironic that his old home is now owned by Fairleigh Dickinson University of New Jersey. An impressive monument to Sir William Pope is to be found near the altar in All Saints church.

HORLEY A collection of golden-brown cottages with thatch and slate roofs set on a south-facing slope. A magnificent wall painting of St Christopher carrying the infant Christ (1450) is to be seen on the north wall of St Etheldreda's church. According to Sherwood and Pevsner, it is "one of the largest and most perfect representations of this saint in the country". Only a tower and chancel survive from the original Norman church - probably built on earlier Saxon foundations.

HORNTON Thatched dwellings of local stone cluster around a small green in the village centre. As in Horley, the church is brightened by outstanding wall paintings. One particularly fine portrait depicts the Black Prince as St George complete with fleur-de-lys. Quarried for centuries from the surrounding countryside, Hornton stone - golden-brown ironstone - is still an important building material in north Oxfordshire and elsewhere.

SHENINGTON A wide variety of rich-brown houses surrounding an extensive hilltop green mark the heart of Shenington. The simple, open church stands east of the green. Victorian restorers moved the superb Norman chancel arch to the north wall where it now frames the organ. The south wall supports a huge red and yellow banner of Shenington Amicable Society (1841 to 1891) - a society which eventually became incorporated into the Independent Order of Oddfellows. Strewing the church with grasses at Whitsuntide is an ancient custom which continues to be performed here each year. The airfield has one claim to fame. From this spot in 1942 Britain's first jet aircraft, the Gloster E28/39 (Meteor prototype) powered by Sir Frank Whittle's historic engine - forerunner of today's jet engines, took to the air on its test flights.

ALKERTON Spread across a western hillside facing Shenington is the hamlet of Alkerton. Beautiful St Michael's church follows the contours, rising up in three levels from nave to altar. Thomas Lydiat, rector here from 1612 to 1646 and tutor to Henry, Prince of Wales, built the adjacent rectory of rich ochre stone in 1625. Brook Cottage gardens, Well Lane, are open to the public during the summer (**Appendix C**).

WALK 3

Broughton Castle
(4¹/₂ miles)

A gentle walk from the attractive village of North Newington across ironstone country to Broughton Castle - a superb 14th century moated manor house, set amidst parkland in a quiet, wooded valley. Elevated parts of the route afford fine views over the local landscape.

O.S. Maps:	Landranger 151. Pathfinder 1045.
Start (419,398):	Park and start at a small green opposite The Blinking Owl pub, North Newington. 2¹/₂ miles W of Banbury on a minor road off the B4035.
Terrain:	Undulating. Eleven stiles.
Refreshments:	North Newington: The Blinking Owl (Free House) 01295-730650 SDA, G, CA, DA. Broughton: Saye and Sele Arms (Lord Saye and Sele) 01295-263348 SDA, G, CA, DA in G. Broughton Castle: tearoom for visitors when the castle is open (**Appendix C**).
Public Transport:	From Banbury: 53(CV) Tu; 55(CV) W.

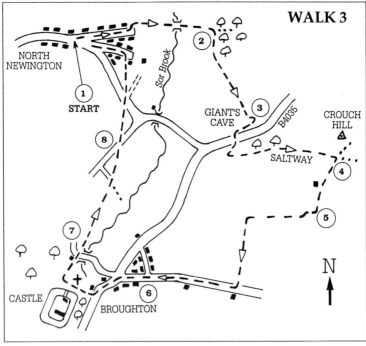

Route:

1.   From the village green walk down School Lane. At the end, bear left over a stile and climb a farm track to a second stile. On the far side, turn right. Go along the edge of a paddock and soon cross a third stile. Our track now descends to the far left-hand corner of a pasture. Pass over a stile and proceed in the same direction along the right-hand side of an arable field. When the field comes to an end, cross two concrete bridges over Sor Brook. Continue forwards on a well-trodden path beside the left-hand boundary of the next field to reach a plantation of young trees.

2.   The track forks here. Take the right-hand track leading uphill along the field edge (part of the Banbury Fringe Circular Walk). Enjoy fine views of North Newington from the field corner. Follow the path as it swings left through trees and then right into the next field. Walk on an undulating track beside the right-hand field boundary. Broughton village can be seen over the hedge on your right. Later on, Crouch Hill (550ft, 169m), the highest point in the area, becomes visible on the left. After descending through trees, the track splits into several paths at an area of hillocks and scrubland known as The Bretch or Giant's Cave. According to legend a secret tunnel ran from the cave to Broughton Castle; it was supposedly used by plotters during the Civil War.

3.   Take the left-hand path along the field edge. In 25 yards turn right at a waymarked wooden post and go down a flight of steps. Cross a tarmacked car park to a similar post visible in the gap ahead. Our route now bears right onto a downhill path running parallel to the B4035 road and in 150 yards comes to a flight of wooden steps over a wall on the left. Cross over the steps and B4035 road. Swing half right onto a broad track. After 150 yards the track turns sharply left and continues between bushes and trees. This is the Salt Way - an ancient road used to convey salt from Droitwich (Worcestershire) to London and the South-East. In ¹/₂ mile look out for Crouch Farm, hiding behind the right-hand hedge. One hundred and fifty yards beyond the farm buildings turn right through a gap in the hedge (marked by a wooden post) and enter a field.

4.   Turn half right and follow a path towards the left-hand corner of the buildings. (If recently ploughed, aim for an electricity pole in

the middle of the field.) The spire of Bloxham church, 2 miles distant, is visible across the fields on your left. Climb a fastened gate on the far side of the field and continue ahead across a pasture - aiming just left of the buildings. Cross a concrete farm drive. Proceed forwards on a grassy track running parallel to the right-hand field boundary, some 25 yards away. The track eventually veers right and comes to another fastened gate. Climb over and go ahead into the next field.

5. In 40 yards our route bears left through a wide gap in a hedge and then immediately right along a field boundary. Follow the path to the far corner. Go through a gap in the hedge ahead, a few yards left of the corner. Swing left and walk for $^1/_3$ mile alongside the hedge to reach a metalled road. Turn right. After a further $^1/_3$ mile arrive at Broughton village.

6. Do not follow the one-way system round to the right but proceed forwards to reach crossroads at the B4035. Cross to the far side and turn left. Walk on the pavement past the Saye and Sele Arms. The path snakes its way downhill, veering right at Warren Lodge onto a wide, flagstone surface which leads over Sor Brook to a churchyard. Go through the churchyard, past the church (open when the castle is open), and out of the far gate into the parkland of BROUGHTON CASTLE. "You are welcome to walk in the park" - so make a diversion here and walk around the moat to view the castle. When your exploration is complete, follow the entrance drive to the Lodge and leave by the main gate. If the gate is locked, use a stone stile on the far side of the Lodge.

7. Turn left. After 10 yards swing right through a gate into a field. Bear half left and walk on a path gradually ascending towards the horizon. (If recently ploughed, aim for the second electricity pole from the left. Beyond the pole, go towards the left-hand end of a line of trees on the horizon.) At the end of the field climb a stile and cross the entrance drive to a sewage works. Climb a second stile. Turn half left and proceed across an arable field to another stile in the far hedge. Cross the stile into a road. Turn right. (If the last field is blocked by crops, turn left along the sewage works drive and then right at a road junction.)

8. In 10 yards turn half left through a wide gap in the left-hand

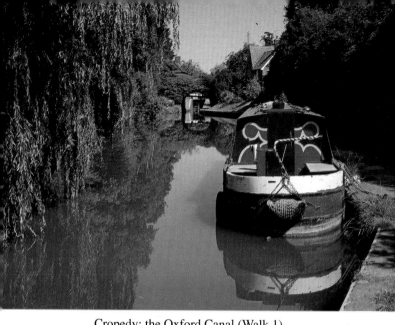

Cropedy: the Oxford Canal (Walk 1)
North Newington (Walk 3)

The Whispering Knights (Walk 5)
The Oxford Canal near Lower Heyford (Walk 8)

Broughton Castle

hedge and continue on a broad track across a field. Look back for a fine view of Broughton church spire rising above the wooded Sor valley. Cross a stile at the field boundary and swing left along a metalled road. After 20 yards turn right over a cattle grid at the entrance to Broughton Farms. Immediately bear half left over parkland to a small, solitary tree a few yards right of an electricity pole. On reaching the tree, veer half right. Walk to the corner of a stone wall and continue ahead, keeping the wall on your left. Cross a stile between gardens and soon enter Park Lane in North Newington. Turn left. Pass some delightful cottages on your way back to the starting point.

Points of Interest

BROUGHTON CASTLE Set on a three-acre island surrounded by four acres of water, Broughton Castle is considered to be the finest medieval manor house in the county. Originally built of local

33

ironstone by John de Broughton in 1300, the house passed into the hands of William of Wykeham, founder of New College Oxford, in 1377. The present owners, the Fiennes family, acquired the property in 1477 when Margaret Wykeham married William Fiennes, 2nd Lord Saye and Sele. Major changes to the fabric in the 16th century saw the addition of a Tudor front and the construction of two new floors above the magnificent Great Hall. The comparatively tiny Council Chamber at the top of the west stairs is of great historic interest. Here, between 1629 and 1640, Pym, Hampden, Essex, William Fiennes and others secretly met to plan their opposition to Charles I - opposition which eventually led to the Civil War. The adjacent church of St Mary contains monuments to owners of the castle from John de Broughton onwards. (See **Appendix C** for opening times).

WALK 4

The Sibfords - Stour Valley
(Walk A 6¹/₂ miles, Walk B 3³/₄ miles)

The twin hilltop villages of Sibford Ferris and Sibford Gower, with their picturesque cottages and unique manor house, form the starting point for this ramble through north-west Oxfordshire. The route follows Ditchedge Lane, a high-level drove-road marking the boundary with Warwickshire, from which there are outstanding views. Walk A continues along the upper Stour valley towards the river's source near Sibford Ferris.

O.S. Maps:	Landranger 151. Pathfinder 1044.
Start (359,374):	Shop/PO in Sibford Ferris. Park here at the side of the road. 7 miles W of Banbury on a minor road off the B4035.
Terrain:	Undulating. Walk A: four stiles. Walk B: no stiles.
Refreshments:	Sibford Gower: The Wykham Arms (Free House) 01295-780351 SDA, G, PA, CA, CM, DA, closed

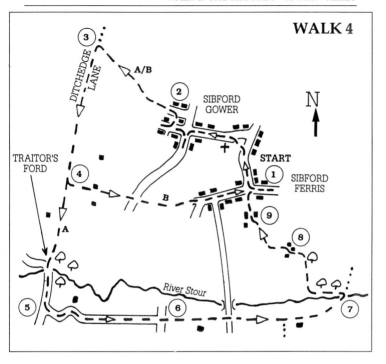

M lunchtime in winter.

Public Transport: From Banbury: 55(CV) W; 480(J, M) M-Sat.

Walk A (6½ miles)
Route:

1.   Walk downhill from SIBFORD FERRIS post office to a road junction in the village centre. Turn right. The road to Sibford Gower winds and dips before climbing steeply into the hamlet of Burdrop. About 30 yards past Bishop Blaize Inn (on your right) turn left through a small wooden gate next to a wooden electricity pole and tall hedge. Follow a tarmac path uphill through a grassy area and between houses to reach a road. Turn left. Immediately pass Holy Trinity church (open) and after ¼ mile come to a crossroads in

Sibford Gower Manor House

SIBFORD GOWER. Turn left. Note the Manor House opposite The Wykham Arms. A little further on, arrive at the entrance drive to a Quaker Meeting House. Climb the drive to find a simple building and unusual burial ground hiding behind trees. Return to the crossroads. Turn left and descend to a delightful spot beside the village pond. Head back towards the crossroads, but in 100 yards bear left onto a signposted footpath beside a cottage. Soon reach a road and swing left.

2.   The road quickly becomes a farm track. After passing Home Farm on the left, go through a gate and continue ahead down the right-hand side of a field. In 200 yards the track descends into a hollow near to a hedge and proceeds through a gate. Clear, sparkling, spring water issues forth from the hillside at this point. Descend across the next field, aiming for a gate beside tall trees in the far left-hand corner. Beyond the gate, cross a stream and climb a tree-lined track. After ¹/₃ mile arrive at a T-junction with Ditchedge Lane. Turn left.

3.   Our route now follows this ancient drove-road. On the way,

superb views open up to Sibford Gower and across the Stour valley. In $^3/_4$ mile the right-hand hedge comes to an end at a metal gate across the track. Twenty-five yards further on, note a second metal gate (used in Walk B) in the hedge on your left.

4.   Continue ahead, passing Lower Atchill Farm on your right. The track gradually descends into a wooded valley. At the valley floor go through a gate and enter a metalled road at Traitor's Ford. Turn left. Vehicles ford the River Stour at this point while walkers cross by a footbridge. Climb up the far side of the valley using a roadside verge and in $^1/_3$ mile come to a T-junction. Bear left on a road to The Sibfords.

5.   For the next 2 miles our route runs parallel to the Stour, steadily ascending the river valley. The roadside verges are generally wide and occasionally shaded by trees. At first, the road winds and undulates past Leys Farm. Beyond the farm, your view to the left encompasses Sibford Ferris and a radio mast near to Epwell. After $^3/_4$ mile arrive at a T-junction.

6.   Walk ahead on a bridleway signposted to Swalcliffe. The gently undulating track soon passes an entrance to Belle Isle Farm and in $^1/_2$ mile comes to a road. Cross to the far side and continue forwards on the bridleway. In 300 yards the main track curves right to a barn, but our path keeps going in the same direction, following a hedge on the right-hand side of the field and a line of electricity poles. When the hedge comes to an end, go ahead across an open field, ignoring a path turning off to the right. Look back for a good view of the Stour valley. We now follow the d'Arcy Dalton Way (**Appendix A**) back to Sibford Ferris. Pass through a gap in a hedge, turn a quarter left and proceed downhill. Arrive at a farm track in the far left-hand field corner. Turn left over a stream - the infant Stour, somewhat reduced in size since Traitor's Ford!

7.   Ten yards past the stream, swing left onto a bridleway through woods. In $^1/_4$ mile the track curves right, crosses a stream and enters a field. Walk uphill along the right-hand field boundary. When the field comes to an end our path re-enters woodland, gradually climbing beside a stream to reach a gate. Go through and follow the left-hand field edge round to the left. Once around the bend, turn a quarter right and strike out across the field to a gate 70 yards away

in the far right-hand corner. Beyond the gate, proceed on a farm track towards the buildings of Sibford Grounds Farm.

8.   Our route follows a zigzag path through the farm buildings, turning left at the first barn and then right, left, right, left at 20-25 yard intervals. It goes beneath electricity and telephone wires to reach a drive in the far right-hand corner of the farm. Walk along the drive (beside phone lines) away from the farm and enjoy wide views over the Stour valley. After $^1/_4$ mile, the phone lines curve off to the right. A few yards further on, at the end of a hedge, turn three-quarters right and take an ascending path across an arable field. If the route is obscure, aim 50 yards to the right of a concrete building on the horizon. Climb a stile on the far side.

9.   A fenced path takes us through the grounds of Sibford School to a tarmac drive. Turn right and walk between school buildings. When the drive passes through a metal gate and curves left, continue ahead over a stile into a field. Follow a downward gradient beside the left-hand field edge to a stile at the bottom. Beyond the stile, descend stone steps to a road junction in the centre of Sibford Ferris. Bear right and retrace your steps to the starting point.

Walk B (3¾ miles)
Route:
Follow Instructions 1-3 of Walk A, to reach point 4 on the map. Turn left through the metal gate. Our path leads across a field to the end of a hedge. It continues beside the hedge, descending along the left-hand side of three fields to reach a metalled road. Cross to the far side. Go through a gate into a pasture and walk alongside the left-hand boundary for 50 yards. Bear a quarter right. Climb across the field to a gate in the far right-hand corner. Beyond the gate, follow the right-hand edge of a second pasture to enter a hedge-lined track. Soon reach a metalled road in Sibford Ferris and turn left. In 200 yards come to a road junction. Go forwards past cottages to a second junction and continue in the same direction back to the starting point.

Points of Interest

SIBFORD FERRIS Attractive ironstone dwellings line the main

street. A former 17th century manor house in the village centre continues to be part of the Quaker School founded here in 1842. The modern school buildings lie beyond trees on the opposite side of the road.

SIBFORD GOWER Originally a group of stone and thatch houses clustered around a pond and crossroads which has, in recent years, extended eastwards to join the hamlet of Burdrop. Of many interesting buildings in the village, the Manor House is the most remarkable. Red-brick chimneys, a flying buttress, a stunning variety of windows and a tower added as a folly in 1910 all form part of this huge, rambling, thatched structure. The flamboyant style of the building exhibits the character of a former owner, Frank Lascelles, who reconstructed the house in the form you see it today, between 1910 and 1915. Sadly it led to his financial ruin. Son of the village vicar, with an abundance of artistic and theatrical talent, he organised spectacular pageants throughout Britain and around the world. A lovely memorial to his mother resides in the south transept of Holy Trinity church. Her gentle face, sculpted by Lascelles, looks out of a bower of roses set in a blue and gold mosaic.

WALK 5

Rollright Stones
($5^{1/}4$ miles)

An undemanding walk from Great Rollright along an ancient Cotswold ridgeway to the Rollright Stones - prehistoric objects of mystery and legend. The route, mostly above 700ft (215m), follows the Oxfordshire/Warwickshire border and offers superb views across both counties.

O.S. Maps:	Landranger 151. Pathfinder 1044.
Start (326,314):	Park and start at the junction of Church End and Tyte End, near Great Rollright church. $2^{1/}2$ miles N of Chipping Norton on a minor road off the A3400.

Terrain:	Mostly level; a few gentle inclines. Five stiles.
Refreshments:	Great Rollright: Wyatt's Farm Shop and Tearooms, daily, 10-6. S.
Public Transport:	From Banbury: 487,488(M) M-Sat.

Route:

1. Starting at GREAT ROLLRIGHT our outward route follows the d'Arcy Dalton Way (**Appendix A**). From its junction with Tyte End, walk upwards along Church End for 100 yards to a right-hand bend. Turn half left here through a wooden kissing gate and take a diagonal path to the far right-hand corner of a pasture. Exit from the pasture into a road (Hemplands). Turn right. In 100 yards note a large stone building on your right with a give-away sign holder jutting out from the first storey. It was once the Unicorn pub. At crossroads turn left along a quiet, shaded road to Long Compton. After ¹/₃ mile the route veers left between white gateposts onto a broad, grassy footpath lined with a hedge and trees.

2. When the trees peter out, enjoy the first of many fine views over Oxfordshire (left) and Warwickshire (right) to be experienced during the course of this walk. At the end of the first field pass through a

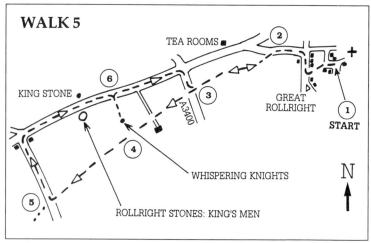

The Rollright Stones: King's Men

wide gap between a hedge and trees. Continue in the same direction across an open field and through a belt of trees before descending a flight of steps to the A3400.

3.   Cross to the far side and swing right. In 20 yards turn sharply left onto a footpath (no signs) rising between trees. At the summit, veer right past a waymarked post and enter a field. A well-trodden track goes forwards along the left-hand side of this field and the right-hand side of the subsequent field to reach a stile. Cross a metalled drive leading to Brighthill Farm. Climb a stile on the far side and walk across an open field to another stile in a hedge. Beyond the hedge look right to the Whispering Knights, some 150 yards away (visited later).

4.   Bear slightly left and proceed on a downward gradient across an open field. A gap in the far hedge leads onto a path descending along the left-hand side of the next field. In the field corner, pass through an opening beside a white gate and enter a metalled road. Turn right.

5.   Look left to see the tiny hamlet of Little Rollright, nestling in the

valley below. Climb $^1/_3$ mile to a crossroads. Turn right. In $^1/_4$ mile arrive at an entrance to the ROLLRIGHT STONES. A small entrance fee is payable by visitors to the stone circle (King's Men). Eighty yards further along the road, climb a stile on the left and enter Warwickshire to view the King Stone. Note also the village of Long Compton about one mile away in the neighbouring valley. Our route continues for 200 yards along the same road to reach a metal gate on the right (no signs). Go through the gate and follow a path to the Whispering Knights. On returning to the road, bear right.

6.   In $^1/_2$ mile come to staggered crossroads at the A3400. If refreshments are required, continue ahead to the Tea Rooms (see map). After being refreshed, walk along the road to Point 2 on the map and retrace your steps to the start. If refreshments are not required, turn right along the A3400. After 200 yards bear left up the flight of steps used earlier and follow the outward route back to Great Rollright.

Points of Interest

GREAT ROLLRIGHT An intriguing mix of Cotswold stone dwellings and modern housing. The church of St Andrew is virtually unaltered since its building between 1100 and 1450. Only the main doorways survive from the earliest period. Decorated with beakheads, medallions and zigzags, the south doorway is considered a gem of Norman craftsmanship. The south arcade and chancel arch remain from the 13th century, while the west tower, clerestory windows and chancel screen were added between 1300 and 1450. On the north wall, 106 different ways of spelling the village name make up the border of an illuminated manuscript. Four memorials are noteworthy: a fine brass in the chancel to James Battersby (1522); the clock to a former rector, Henry Rendall; the attractive lychgate to Mrs Rendall from her nine sons; a tombstone, left of the gate, to Richard Widdows, a shepherd aged 104.

ROLLRIGHT STONES The most important group of prehistoric objects in the county. All are fashioned out of local limestone and eroded by the weather into irregular shapes. Between 70 and 80 standing stones (the exact number cannot be counted, according to local folklore) make up a 100ft (30m) circle known as the King's Men. Sizes range from a few inches to 7ft (2m). One hundred yards north-east, on the opposite side of the ridgeway, stands the huge solitary King Stone overlooking Warwickshire. It may have been a guide stone for travellers from that county. The King Stone and King's Men were probably erected on this site during the Bronze Age, some 3,000 years ago. Their purpose is unknown. The Whispering Knights, 400 yards east of the stone circle, are undoubtedly much older, perhaps by a thousand years. These five large slabs - four uprights and a displaced capping stone - are believed to be the remains of a Neolithic long barrow.

Many legends have grown up around the "Stones". The one most frequently quoted refers to a king who wished to rule the whole of England. Riding along the ridgeway with his army of knights and men, on his way from one battle to the next, he met up with the local witch. As was the practice in those days, he asked her to tell his fortune. She replied:

> "Seven long strides thou shalt take,
> And if Long Compton thou canst see,
> King of England thou shalt be."

Wondering what the outcome of this challenge might be, the knights stood whispering together while the men formed a circle. The king was delighted and strode towards the edge of the ridge. As he took his last stride a mound of earth rose up to block his view and the cackling witch was heard to proclaim:

> "As Long Compton thou canst not see,
> King of England thou shalt not be.
> Rise up, stick, and stand still, stone,
> For King of England thou shalt be none.
> Thou and thy men hoar stones shall be,
> And I myself an eldern tree."

WALK 6

South Newington - Great Tew

(6¹/₂ miles)

Great Tew, one of the prettiest villages in the county, is the focal point of this walk. Setting out from South Newington, the southward path soon reveals extensive panoramas of the surrounding countryside. Two fine churches and the Great Tew estate provide an absorbing historical background while an award winning pub is on hand to supply refreshments. (N.B. The outward route passes through a field beside Grove Ash Farm which contains a bull and cows from June to September each year. Notices are posted on the field gates.)

O.S. Maps:	Landranger 151, 164. Pathfinder 1045, 1068, 1069.
Start (407,333):	Park and start at South Newington church. 5¹/₂ miles SW of Banbury on the A361.
Terrain:	Undulating. No stiles.
Refreshments:	Great Tew: The Falkland Arms (Free House) 01608-683653 SDA, G, CA inside when food is being served, DA in G and flagged area, normal pub hours but closed M lunchtime, food: Tu-Sat 12-2. S.
Public Transport:	From Banbury: 487,488(M) M-Sat; 55(CV) W; 8, 9(P) Th.

Route:

1. With your back to the church walk forwards, up SOUTH NEWINGTON High Street. Cross over a road at the far end and go ahead on a gently rising bridleway to Great Tew. At the summit, where the main track veers left, continue forwards on a path descending between trees. In 200 yards our route goes through a wooden gate, turns right for 30 yards and enters a field. Follow a grassy track beside the left-hand hedge. When the track veers right,

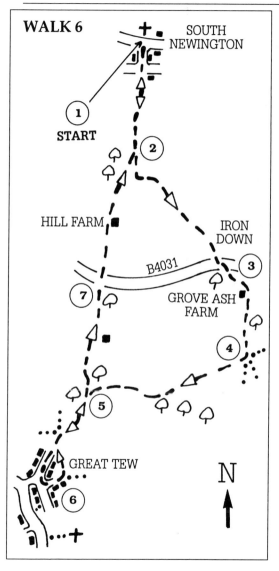

keep alongside the field boundary and pass through a wide gap in a hedge. Continue beside the left edge of the next field. Hill Farm comes into view on the forward horizon near to the end of this field.

2. One hundred yards before reaching the field corner turn left through a gate. Walk along the left-hand side of the adjacent field for 150 yards to a point where the field boundary swings half left. An underground stream bursts forth beneath a pollarded

45

ash tree at this spot. Turn right. Go across the field and through a metal gate on the far side. Ignore a farm track going ahead. Instead, turn a quarter left and climb towards the tallest clump of bushes on the horizon. At the crest of the hill (Iron Down) look back for a superb panorama across the Swere valley. Note Bloxham church spire (3 miles north-east) and a radio mast in Banbury ($5^{1}/_{2}$ miles distant and left of the spire). Pass through a metal gate and follow a hedge running along the left-hand side of the next field. When the hedge comes to an end, continue ahead on a grassy track between fields to arrive at the B4031.

3.   Turn left. After 100 yards branch right onto a metalled lane winding downhill to Grove Ash Farm. Turn left at the farmhouse. Go along a cart track around a barn to reach a gate across the track. The walk continues through the gate and along the right-hand edge of a long field, passing close to a wooded slope (Raven Hill) on your left. When the right-hand field boundary veers right, follow the path forwards to a wooden gate. Walk through the next field for 70 yards to arrive at a staggered crossing of tracks.

4.   Turn right. A stony farm track (Groveash Lane) proceeds across an open field and then between hedges and trees. After $^{3}/_{4}$ mile, notice a radio mast atop a hill on your left overlooking cottages in Great Tew. In a further $^{1}/_{4}$ mile come to a T-junction. Turn left.

5.   The track goes through woods and parkland for $^{1}/_{3}$ mile to another junction. Follow the main route as it swings left and climbs past Park Farm to reach the first thatched house in GREAT TEW (Bee Bole Cottage). The track becomes a metalled lane ascending beside picturesque dwellings to the village centre. To see more of the village, including the church, $^{1}/_{3}$ mile away, walk past The Falkland Arms and some delightful cottages. Note a date of 1636 carved on the near gable-end of those on your left. In 100 yards turn right onto a narrow gravel path climbing along the far side of the right-hand cottages. Come to a road and turn left. Pass the entrance to Great Tew Park on your left and the old blacksmith's workshop, with its central archway, on the right. After $^{1}/_{4}$ mile arrive at an ornate stone gateway to St Michael's church, opposite the old vicarage.

6.   When your exploration is complete, return to The Falkland

Arms. Take a bridleway alongside the pub going past Hornbeam House. Soon reach the Square - an area of gardens enclosed on three sides by cottages. Turn left opposite No. 49 - a home decorated with horse and ox shoes rescued from local fields. Pass more cottages and go through a gate into a pasture. Follow a downward path across the pasture to Brookside Cottage. At the cottage, bear left along a track beside a stream. The track soon merges with a farm drive. After 120 yards come to Bee Bole Cottage - our original point of entry into the village. Turn right. The walk now retraces the outward journey to point 5 on the map; it then continues ahead for $^3/_4$ mile past Cottenham Farm to the B4031.

7.   Cross the road and go up a drive to Hill Farm. Opposite the first building (a house) bear half left through a metal gate and walk across a field to the far end of a barn. At the barn, turn half right. Follow the back of the building and continue in the same direction along a farm track. Pass a wooden electricity post. Go through a gap in the far hedge and turn right. In 100 yards arrive at a metal gate. Do not go through, but swing left onto a track running alongside a barbed wire fence. More magnificent views of North Oxfordshire are to be had from this track. Pass through a gate in the field corner and quickly descend between fences. When the fences come to an end, proceed in the same direction across an open field to reach a hedge on the far side. This is point 2 on the map. Turn half left alongside the hedge and retrace your steps back to South Newington.

Points of Interest

SOUTH NEWINGTON Early records show the village as a Saxon settlement, probably at a convenient ford over the River Swere. Nowadays, a busy A361 bypasses the quiet, charming High Street of ironstone cottages leading from the church of St Peter ad Vincula. The church is kept locked but keys can be obtained from College Farm (next door) or the Old Vicarage (across the road). Built in three stages during the 12th-15th centuries, St Peter's contains "the finest group of medieval wall paintings in the county" (Sherwood and Pevsner). One set (North Aisle), executed in oils on plaster about 1350, includes: the martyrdom of Beckett; a unique portrayal of the martyrdom of Thomas Lancaster; Virgin and Child; and St Margaret slaying a dragon. A second set, in a late 15th century rustic style,

*Great Tew:
gateway to
St Michael's
church*

decorates the nave.

GREAT TEW Enfolded by trees in a secluded valley, thatched, honey-brown cottages lead past the pub and school to Great Tew Park. As you see it today, the village owes much to John Loundon who managed the estate in the 19th century; it was he who created the parkland setting. Don't fail to look inside the 17th century Falkland Arms - a pub which has won UK awards for Village Pub of the Year and Best Bar Interior. It is named after the Falkland family, former owners of the estate, whose most famous son, Lucius Cary, 2nd Lord Falkland, inherited the title in 1625. An intellectual by nature, he kept open house at the manor for scholars from Oxford. During those years before the Civil War, Falkland entered Parliament becoming Secretary of State to Charles I. In spite of his

48

support for the rights of Parliament, he remained loyal to Charles during the war, losing his life at the first Battle of Newbury in 1643. His body rests beneath the chancel of St Michael and All Angels in a peaceful corner of Great Tew Park.

The church, a spacious structure built between 1100 and 1500, is approached along a lovely, laurel-lined path. A monument on the south wall of the chancel records the events of Cary's life. Nearby lies a gracious marble sculpture of Mary Ann Boulton, carved by Sir Francis Chantrey in 1834. There are also some fine brasses including one of Sir John and Lady Wilcote (1410), previous owners of the estate, which can be seen by rolling back the chancel carpet.

WALK 7

Hethe - Cottisford
(Walk A 6³/₄ miles, Walk B 3¹/₄ miles)

This walk along pleasant field paths explores "Flora Thompson Country" - that remote corner of north-east Oxfordshire brought into prominence by the writer's fascinating account of rural life here in the 19th century. From Hethe, a quiet village of thatch and stone, both routes visit the straggling settlement of Cottisford ("Fordlow"). Tusmore House, with its beautiful parkland, and the hamlet of Juniper Hill ("Lark Rise") are also included in the longer route.

O.S. Maps:	Landranger 164, 152. Pathfinder 1069, 1045.
Start (594,295):	Village green and war memorial, Hethe (pronounced "heath"). Park around the green. 4 miles N of Bicester on a minor road off the A421.
Terrain:	Mostly level. Walk A: seven stiles. Walk B: six stiles.
Refreshments:	Juniper Hill: The Fox (Free House) 01869-810616 G, CA, DA in G, phone to check pub is open in winter.
Public Transport:	Bicester-Brackley 37(M) M, W, F.

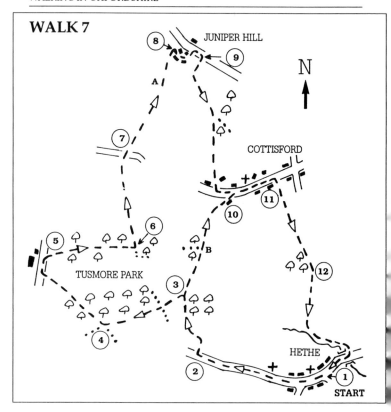

WALK 7

JUNIPER HILL

COTTISFORD

TUSMORE PARK

HETHE

START

Walk A (6¾ miles)

Route:

1.   Before setting out from HETHE it is well worthwhile exploring the village centre. Then return to the war memorial and walk westwards through the village, passing the Whitmore Arms on your right. At a road junction, keep to the main road (signposted "Hardwick"). When the houses come to an end, continue on the footpath as far as a church and then along the grass verge. After ¹/₂ mile turn right onto a signposted bridleway ("Cottisford 1").

2.   At first the wide grassy track is enclosed by hedges but the left hedge soon gives way to open fields. In ¹/₄ mile pass a wood (Fox Covert) on the right and arrive at a T-junction with a farm track.

3.   Turn left. Proceed to the far end of a field. Go straight over a crossing of tracks onto a deeply rutted, grassy pathway. Tusmore Wood, carpeted by bluebells in spring, is on the right. In ¹/₃ mile reach another crossing of tracks and turn right into the wood.

4.   Our route now passes down a broad avenue, lined with yew trees. It continues ahead (via a gate) across open parkland and along an avenue of limes. When the trees come to an end, bear left through a wooden gate to enter a metalled drive. Turn right. In 50 yards arrive at TUSMORE HOUSE - a modest building standing behind magnificent wrought iron gates.

5.   One hundred yards further on, swing right through a wooden gate marked with blue arrows. Walk ahead on a track across open parkland and after ¹/₃ mile pass through a gate at the far side. Continue in the same direction. There is now a wood (Park Plantation) on your left and an open field on the right. At the field corner, where the track veers right, go forwards on a grassy path. In 30 yards reach a tall deer fence. Turn left.

6.   Walk alongside the fence through Park Plantation. When the fence turns right, maintain course over a footbridge. Continue ahead along the right-hand edge of a field and after ¹/₂ mile arrive at a T-junction with a farm track. Turn right. Soon pass through a gate and cross to the far side of a metalled road.

7.   Our route continues forwards on a signposted footpath ("Juniper ¹/₂"). After 10 yards the track goes through a gap in the hedge and follows the right-hand side of a field to reach a stream. Buildings of Heath Farm can be seen on your left, and beyond them, the dish-shaped aerials of RAF Croughton. Cross the stream and proceed along the right-hand edge of the next field. After ¹/₃ mile pass through a gap in a hedge onto an unmade road in the hamlet of JUNIPER HILL.

8.   Turn right. In 150 yards come to two cottages on the right-hand side. Queenie's, the home of "Queenie Massey" in Flora Thompson's books, lies alongside the road. A tiny white cottage behind Queenie's, with a small plaque on the wall, is the remaining half of End House

- where Flora grew up. Walk past the cottages and allotments. After 150 yards swing left onto a grassy path. At the far end of a bungalow, bear left again and follow a track to reach a metalled road. The Fox pub is on your left.

9.   Turn right. In 100 yards branch right through a gate onto a signposted footpath ("Cottisford 1"). After a further 200 yards climb a stile into an open field. The route now proceeds half left along a well-trodden path to reach a belt of trees in the far left-hand corner. (If the field has recently been ploughed, aim slightly left of a group of buildings visible in the distance.) The path forks here. Take the right fork over a stream and onto a track ascending along the left-hand edge of a field. In $^1/_3$ mile enter a metalled road at the western edge of COTTISFORD. Turn left. After 300 yards the road curves left past College Farm.

10.   One hundred and fifty yards further on, arrive at St Mary's - the church attended by Flora Thompson. On leaving the church, turn left. Continue through this scattered settlement, passing Cottisford House and a pond before reaching the old manor buildings (on your right). At the end of the buildings, turn right onto a signposted footpath ("Hethe $1^1/_2$"). Before doing so, you may wish to see the school which Flora attended. If this is the case, walk along the road for 200 yards to a red post box and telephone kiosk. The building on the right at this point, with a tall red-brick chimney, is the old school. It is now a private house. Retrace your steps to the main route.

11.   Proceed through a small wooden gate and garden to reach a stile. Beyond the stile, walk along the right-hand edge of a narrow meadow. Go through a gate in the far right-hand corner and climb an adjacent stile into a marshy area, beneath trees. Turn right. After 5 yards swing left. Make your way through a gap in a line of tall bushes. The route now crosses a stream and stile before bearing half left onto a well-used path over an open field. If the track is not visible, aim halfway between two wooden electricity poles. At the far side, go through a gap in a hedge and along the right-hand side of the next field. Pass a small wood (Windmill Hook) on your right.

12.   When the path divides at the end of Windmill Hook, take the right fork and continue to the end of the field. The tiny spire of Hethe church is visible ahead. Cross a stile into the next field. The path now

proceeds along a valley beside a stream and crosses two more stiles before entering a metalled road in Hethe. Turn right. Go over a bridge and soon arrive back at the starting point.

Walk B (3¼ miles)

Route:

Follow Instructions 1 and 2 of Walk A, to reach point 3 on the map. At the T-junction turn right and walk along a farm track for ¹/₂ mile. Pass College Farm before entering a metalled road in COTTISFORD. Turn right. Now follow Walk A from Instruction 10.

Points of Interest

HETHE A tiny village set on a ridge beside a stream. Attractive thatched, tiled and slate-roofed dwellings cluster round the village green, war memorial and "Hethe Town Well". A large oak and two chestnuts lead to a second green lined with more attractive dwellings.

TUSMORE HOUSE The modest neo-Georgian house (1965) seen today replaced a truly majestic Georgian house built in 1770 for the Fermor family. Splendid parkland, gardens and an ornamental lake survive from the earlier house; a temple of peace is a memorial to the poet Pope, a friend of the Fermors, who made Arabella Fermor the heroine of his poem *The Rape of the Lock*.

JUNIPER HILL Established in the mid-18th century to house the poor, it became the birthplace and youthful home of Flora Thompson. Life here in the 1880s is lovingly recalled in her famed trilogy *Larkrise to Candleford*. Nowadays Juniper Hill ("Larkrise") is no larger than it was in the 19th century - a few cottages and The Fox, the latter disguised as "The Waggon and Horses" in the books.

COTTISFORD The "Fordlow" of Thompson's trilogy also remains today almost exactly as it was in the 1880s - a single street whose "few buildings were strung out along the roadside, so far between and so sunken in greenery that there seemed no village at all". The Early English church of St Mary, much restored in Victorian times, retains a fine 13th century porch. Above the pew used by Flora and her brother Edwin is a First World War Memorial; tragically Edwin's name is the final entry. To the left is a 1995 memorial to Flora.

WALK 8
Steeple Aston - Rousham
(5¹/₄ miles)

A ramble through a beautiful stretch of the Cherwell valley north of
Lower Heyford. The first section follows the Oxford Canal as far as
Upper Heyford before ascending to the attractive village of Steeple
Aston. The return via field and woodland paths affords fine views
of Rousham House and Park.

O.S. Maps:	Landranger 164. Pathfinder 1069.
Start (486,248):	Market Square, Lower Heyford. Park here near to The Bell Inn or in Church Lane. 9 miles S of Banbury on the B4030.
Terrain:	Mostly level with a few gentle inclines. Five stiles.
Refreshments:	Steeple Aston: Red Lion (Free House) 01869-340225 G, CA in G and restaurant, DA if small; drinks: M-Sat 11-3, 6-11, Sun 7-10.30; bar meals M-Sat 11-3, restaurant 6-11 Tu-Sat; closed two weeks Sept/Oct. S.
Public Transport:	Rail: To Heyford from Banbury and Oxford (TT) M-Sat. Bus: Banbury-Oxford X58, X59(M) M-Sat; Bicester-Oxford 34, X57(M) M-Sat.

Route:

1.   From LOWER HEYFORD Market Square go past The Bell into
Freehold Street. Turn left. Walk for 300 yards along a picturesque
street of ironstone cottages before branching left down Mill Lane.
Soon cross a metal bridge over the OXFORD CANAL (**Walk 1** and
Appendix A) and swing right along the towpath. After 200 yards
the Cherwell appears on your left. For the next mile this delightful
path resting on a narrow spit of land between river and canal
meanders through meadow and field. In ³/₄ mile the ancient tithe
barn and church tower of Upper Heyford are seen on the far bank.

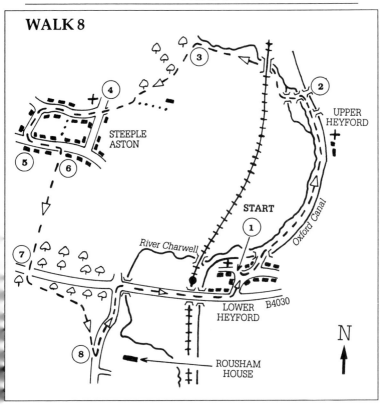

WALK 8

Pass Allen's Lock with its associated bridge. Two hundred yards further on, climb a stile on the left-hand side of a second bridge.

2.   Turn left. Immediately cross a bridge over a branch of the Cherwell and bear right along the riverside. In 100 yards veer left. Cross a second bridge over another branch of the Cherwell and swing right to walk beside the river. River and footpath soon pass under bridges carrying the Oxford-Banbury railway line. Beyond the bridges, proceed forwards on a track across a meadow going towards woodland. The Cherwell makes a large loop at this point before renewing contact with our path, halfway across the meadow.

Continue along the river bank until you are 80 yards short of the woodland. Turn left here. Cross the meadow to a stile and footbridge on the far side.

3.   Beyond the footbridge walk through a narrow belt of trees before climbing straight ahead across an open field. Aim for the left end of a line of trees ahead, keeping parallel to the left-hand field boundary. Go through a gap in a hedge to experience one of the surprises of Oxfordshire - the Rousham Eyecatcher. Standing in the next field is a sham ruin built by William Kent to terminate the view along the Cherwell valley from Rousham House, some 2,000 yards distant. Being a mere 200 yards away, the visual impact is ten times larger than intended for residents of the big house! Bear right and follow a path around the field edge. Pass through a metal gate at the end. Turn right onto an unmade lane and walk uphill into STEEPLE ASTON.

4.   At a T-junction in the village, cross over to visit the church on the far side. After your visit, bear right along Northside and enjoy the wide variety of mostly ironstone buildings which make up this fascinating village. In $^1/_4$ mile turn left into Water Lane. The lane crosses a valley before reaching the Red Lion.

5.   Turn left here into Southside. After 250 yards arrive at two footpath signs on opposite sides of the road. Thirty yards further on (at Radley Cottage) swing right into a metalled lane.

6.   Our walk now follows a gentle uphill gradient out of Steeple Aston. Look back from the summit for a fine view of the village. When a hedge on the left comes to an end, continue ahead towards a pair of electricity poles. The path descends between open fields, affording fine views over the Cherwell valley to Upper and Lower Heyford. After $^1/_3$ mile come to the woodlands of Dean Plantation. Pass through a few trees and veer right for 20 yards to a stile. Cross into a field. Aim for another stile in the far left-hand corner.

7.   Go over the stile and across a busy road. The track climbs up a wooded bank for 80 yards before turning left to join a shaded path descending beneath horse chestnut trees. At the end of the wood, climb a stile on the right into a large field. Our route (not visible on the ground) goes diagonally across the field to the far right-hand corner. First, aim for the left-hand edge of a group of mature lime

Rousham eyecatcher

trees; then pass around a plantation of younger trees. On your way across the field, look left for good views of Lower Heyford and ROUSHAM PARK. At the field corner, slip through a narrow gap between metal posts next to a gate.

8.   Swing sharply left. Walk on the road beside Rousham Park, using the grass verge where possible. In $^1/_3$ mile arrive at crossroads. Turn right here and cross a bridge over the Cherwell. A short distance further on, look right for an excellent view of Rousham House. Soon cross railway and canal bridges before re-entering Lower Heyford. Turn left at a "Lower Heyford only" sign to reach the starting point.

Points of Interest

LOWER HEYFORD The name "Heyford" comes from a ford across the Cherwell, used especially at hay-making time. Parts of a stone bridge, which had replaced the ford by the late 13th century, are incorporated into the south side of the present structure carrying the B4030 road. The presence of a market square is a sign that the village once had ambitions of becoming a market town. A market did flourish here in the late 19th century but it is no more. Nowadays, a picturesque collection of ironstone cottages grouped around two quiet streets, a pub, a 14th century church and a fine rectory comprise the heart of Lower Heyford. Nearby, colourful longboats lie at berth on the Oxford Canal.

STEEPLE ASTON Stepel is an ancient name for an unfortified tower - a structure which undoubtedly stood here before the present tower of St Peter's. The church, mostly built between the 12th and 15th centuries, is set in a commanding position overlooking the Cherwell valley. Its most impressive monuments are white marble effigies of Sir Francis and Lady Page. Known as the "Hanging Judge", Sir Francis sentenced more than 100 men to death during his lifetime. Photographs of the church's most valuable possession - a rare 14th century embroidered cope - hang by the south door. These days, the cope is stored in the Victoria and Albert Museum. In the churchyard stands one of England's largest sycamore trees - a giant with a girth of 24ft (7.3m).

ROUSHAM PARK Although possessing a fine Jacobean house, built by Sir Robert Dormer in 1635, Rousham is famous for its gardens. Virtually unchanged since they were created between 1738 and 1740 by William Kent - architect, landscape gardener and designer of Horse Guards in London - the gardens embody the first stage of English landscape design. Paths curving through groves revealing classical surprises at every turn, lawns, streams, ponds, cascades, medieval Heyford Bridge, the River Cherwell and distant eyecatchers all form part of Kent's masterpiece. (See **Appendix C**.)

WALK 9

Shipton-under-Wychwood
(6¹/₄ miles)

A pleasant, undemanding walk through the Evenlode valley in the eastern Cotswolds. Heading north-west from the village of Shipton-under-Wychwood a pastoral route leads to the woodlands of Foxholes Nature Reserve. Time can be spent here enjoying the flora and fauna. Our return along the Oxfordshire Way goes past Bruern

Abbey and commands wide views over the river valley and outlying hills.

O.S. Maps:	Landranger 163. Pathfinder 1091, 1068.
Start (279,179):	Village green, Shipton-under-Wychwood. Park in Church Street alongside the green. 6 miles S of Chipping Norton on the A361.
Terrain:	Level and gentle inclines. Two stiles.
Refreshments:	Shipton-under-Wychwood: The Shaven Crown Hotel (Private) 01993-830330 G, CA, DA, normal hours and afternoon tea 3.30-5.30, Sun.
Public Transport:	Rail: From Oxford (GW, TT), M-Sat. (More frequent service to Kingham, $1^{1}/_{2}$ miles N of Foxholes by foot). Bus: From Witney 14, 20(V) Tu, Th.

Route:

1. Walk to the A361 and turn left. Follow the road as it winds its way through SHIPTON-UNDER-WYCHWOOD. After $^{1}/_{4}$ mile look out for Shipton Court, standing beyond open gates on the left. Beyond Shipton Court the road turns right, and in a further 100 yards, left. Continue straight ahead at this point along a signposted footpath to Milton-under-Wychwood. A broad track enclosed by trees soon becomes a hedged path between fields, affording good views over the mosaic of woods and fields which make up the Evenlode valley. In $^{1}/_{2}$ mile the track turns half right (blue arrow here). It then follows a field boundary down to a stream before crossing two fields and entering a metalled road in Milton-under-Wychwood. Go forwards past houses for 300 yards to reach a T-junction. Turn right.

2. Walk past a Baptist Chapel. After 30 yards bear left onto a signposted bridleway between houses. For the next $^{2}/_{3}$ mile our route follows a line of wooden electricity poles across three fields and along a farm track before coming to a metalled lane at Grange Farm.

3. Turn right. A quiet lane, partially shaded by trees, leads us northwards for $^{3}/_{4}$ mile to a road junction. Continue ahead on the road to Bruern. After 100 yards swing left through a small wooden gate onto a bridleway ("Bould 1").

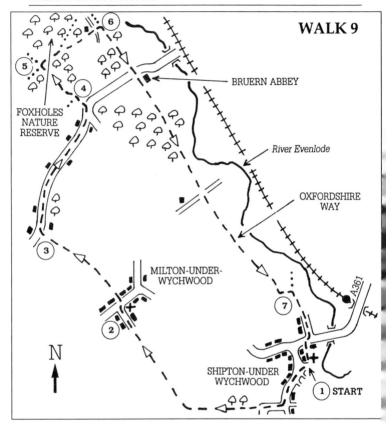

WALK 9

BRUERN ABBEY

FOXHOLES NATURE RESERVE

River Evenlode

OXFORDSHIRE WAY

MILTON-UNDER-WYCHWOOD

N

SHIPTON-UNDER WYCHWOOD

1 START

4. Go straight ahead over an open field and through a gap in a hedge on the far side. The bridleway, which may not be visible on the ground, turns a quarter left across the next field, passing round the left-hand edge of some Scots pines. Aim for a point 70 yards right of the distant, left-hand field corner. (If the way is blocked by crops, walk around the left-hand field edge to reach the same point.) A well used track now goes forwards through a belt of trees. It continues in the same direction across a third field and into the woods of FOXHOLES NATURE RESERVE. Two hundred yards

into the woods arrive at a crossing of bridleways beside a reserve noticeboard.

5.   Turn right. After 300 yards the track divides. Take the right fork following the edge of the woods. Soon pass buildings on your left and cross a farm track before coming to a small car park. A noticeboard describing the nature reserve is situated here. Continue in the same direction, descending through woods past the car park. In 60 yards arrive at a crossing of paths. To view the Evenlode, go ahead over a stile into a meadow. Otherwise, turn right onto the Oxfordshire Way (**Appendix A**) which follows the meandering Evenlode and takes us back to Shipton.

6.   At first, the route is a shaded path through woods - where bluebells bring a splash of colour to the springtime scene. Beyond the woods, our track follows a field edge before crossing a road into parkland. BRUERN ABBEY is close by on the left. Proceed over the parkland and across an open field to reach the start of a ride through Bruern Wood. Look back for an excellent view of the abbey. Continue to the end of the ride; then cross four fields and a fenced track. Good panoramic views of the Evenlode valley and surrounding hills are to be had from this path. On approaching Shipton, the route veers left alongside a hedge to reach a farm track.

7.   Turn right. Soon arrive at the edge of Shipton. Continue forwards along a metalled road and come to the A361. Turn right. After 80 yards turn left down Church Path. Pass the church and enter Church Street. Our starting point is a short distance to the right.

Points of Interest

SHIPTON-UNDER-WYCHWOOD A village in the once royal forest of Wychwood where kings have hunted deer since Saxon times. Buildings of golden Cotswold stone extend around a splendid green and along a winding High Street. Overlooking one side of the green is the elegant, 13th century octagonal spire of St Mary's church; on the opposite side stands the Shaven Crown hotel. Built in the 15th century as a guest-house for Bruern Abbey, the Shaven Crown retains many original features: an arched gateway, a hall with a double-collar braced roof and a courtyard. For some years after the Dissolution, Elizabeth I used the building as a hunting lodge.

Shipton Court

A Victorian drinking fountain, across the road from the hotel, tells a tragic tale. It was erected in "memory of 17 parishioners who perished in the *Cospatrick* by fire on her voyage to New Zealand" in 1874. Of the 477 emigrants who set out from Gravesend, only three survived.

At the end of an avenue of clipped yews leading off the High Street stands Shipton Court - a magnificent Jacobean house. Built in 1603 for the Lacy family it is one of the largest houses in England to survive from this period.

FOXHOLES NATURE RESERVE A BBONT (Berkshire, Buckinghamshire and Oxfordshire Naturalists' Trust) reserve of 158 acres comprising a wide range of habitats. Visitors are welcome. The area is mostly deciduous woodland - a remnant of Wychwood Forest - but also includes a wet meadow sloping down to the River Evenlode. Wildlife seen in the reserve includes foxes, muntjac and fallow deer, adders, grass snakes, more than twenty species of butterfly and an abundance of birds. Woodland flora include bluebells, primroses, orchids, wild angelica, sanicle and goldilocks buttercup, while great burnet and devils'-bit scabious flourish in the wet meadow.

BRUERN ABBEY Nothing now remains of the original 12th century Cistercian foundation. The present house (1720), built in local Baroque style for the Cope family, underwent modifications in the 1970s including the addition of a new north façade. Nowadays the building is home to a boarding school.

WALK 10

Charlbury - Wychwood Forest
(Walk A 9 miles, Walk B 7¹/₄ miles)

On its journey from the Cotswolds to the Thames the Evenlode makes a great loop around the high ground of Wychwood Forest. Half of this walk follows elevated terrain along the loop, giving distant views across the eastern Cotswold hills. The remainder explores a lovely part of the medieval forest, where deer still roam.

O.S. Maps:	Landranger 164. Pathfinder 1091, 1068.
Start (358,196):	Park and start at the Spendlove Centre, Charlbury. 5¹/₂ miles SE of Chipping Norton on the B4022.
Terrain:	Both walks: Level and gentle inclines; five stiles.
Refreshments:	Charlbury: a wide range available. Finstock: The Plough Inn (Free House) 01993-868333 SDA, G, PΛ, CΛ, DΛ. S.
Public Transport:	Rail: From Oxford (GW, TT) daily. Bus: From Oxford 70 (WO) M-Sat; from Witney 69/71 (WO) M-Sat.

Walk A (9 miles)

Route:

1.   Leave the car park and turn right into Brown's Lane. In 150 yards reach a crossroads. Proceed to the far side and continue ahead down Church Street. When Church Street veers left, go forwards through an iron gate into the churchyard. Our route follows a path past the church and into Church Lane on the far side. Walk to the

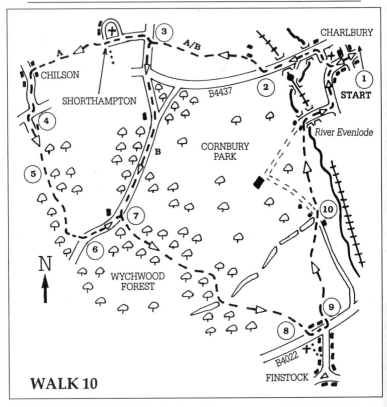

WALK 10

end of Church Lane; turn left and descend out of CHARLBURY.
Soon cross river and railway bridges. Charlbury Station, a listed
building designed by Brunel, is on your left.

2.   Two hundred yards beyond the railway bridge branch right
onto a narrow road, signposted "Walcot only". Look right for a
good view of Charlbury. After 1/4 mile pass through the hamlet of
Walcot and proceed ahead on a farm track ("Bridleway to Chilson").
Continue for 3/4 mile to reach a road. On the way, enjoy fine views
over the Evenlode valley - a patchwork of fields, woods and
scattered villages.

Blenheim Palace and Queen Pool (Walk 11)
The Grand Bridge, Blenheim Park (Walk 11)

Water crowfoot growing on the River Cherwell (Walk 12)
Minster Lovell Old Hall (Walk 16)

3. Turn right. In 20 yards go left down a lane to SHORTHAMPTON. When the road divides, take the right fork and soon come to the tiny church of All Saints - a little gem amongst Oxfordshire churches. The door latch is stiff, so press hard! After experiencing the special charm of this place, retrace your steps to the fork. Turn right. When the road curves right, proceed forwards on a farm track, ignoring a signposted footpath to the left. In $^3/_4$ mile arrive at Chilson. Turn left. Walk through this picturesque village - most colourful in spring when the daffodils are in flower. Continue on the far side to reach the B4437. Turn right. After 50 yards go left into a lane signposted "Chilson Hill only".

4. Beyond the cottages of Chilson Hill, our route becomes a grassy track which winds its way around an old orchard. The path keeps to the left-hand edge of a field, gradually climbing uphill towards woodland on the horizon. Yellow arrows mark the route. Before passing through a gap in a hedge at the top of the field, look back for a final panorama of the Evenlode valley. Carry on in the same direction, passing a narrow wood on the left before entering deciduous woodland.

5. The route is now a farm track. In 100 yards this track veers left, but our path goes straight ahead on an upward gradient. The deciduous woodland eventually gives way to conifers. When the conifers come to an end, you reach a T-junction with another path. Turn left. After 25 yards go right and walk downhill through an open area of mature conifers and young trees. Trees on the left are soon replaced by a field. Our track follows round the edge of this field to reach a quiet road. Turn left.

6. Walk on the grass verge and in $^1/_2$ mile come to Waterman's Lodge Farm. Turn right opposite the farm drive. Go over a stile onto a footpath through WYCHWOOD FOREST, signposted "Finstock 2".

7. Yellow arrows mark our route through the forest. A wide path slowly descends through oak, beech and other deciduous species to join a broad, grassy ride running along a valley bottom. When the valley comes to an end at a wide open area (part of the Grand Vista of Cornbury House), the path veers half right into woodland. After passing a sawmill, the route drops down to a small lake on the right

fed by springs. Turn left here. Walk uphill through trees to a gate. Go through and follow an undulating track for the next $^2/_3$ mile to arrive at the B4022 road in Finstock.

8. If you do not wish to visit The Plough, turn left and keep to a grass verge beside the road. Now go to Instruction 9. To visit The Plough, continue ahead across the road onto an unmade lane alongside a churchyard. When the churchyard comes to an end, the lane narrows down to a path beside a field. At a housing estate proceed forwards, keeping a row of garages on your left. Swing left at a T-junction and in 100 yards arrive at School Road. Turn right. Drop down into "The Bottom" to find The Plough. Return through the village via School Road and turn right at the B4022.

9. One hundred yards past The Crown pub, bear left over a stone stile onto a footpath signposted "Charlbury $1^1/_2$". Go through a gap in a hedge. Turn half right across a lawn to a large wooden gate next to a derelict building. Pass through the gate and proceed ahead on a descending farm track. After $^1/_2$ mile continue to follow the track as it turns right around the corner of a field. Walk downhill past young trees alongside a wooden fence. In 100 yards, when the fence curves away to the left, branch half left off the farm track and go downhill along a wide avenue lined with trees. Yellow arrows mark the route. Cross another farm track and continue forwards on a fenced footpath to a metalled drive beside Park Farm. Turn left.

10. Walk over a dam at the end of a lake and veer right into the Fishery Car Park. Our path now follows a tall deer fence, first along the left-hand side of the car park, and then between trees. Good views into CORNBURY PARK are to be had from this path, with occasional glimpses of Cornbury House. A small stone building beneath the trees is an icehouse. The track continues for $^1/_2$ mile, crossing three stiles on the way, to reach an entrance drive to Cornbury Park at North Lodge. Turn right. Cross two bridges and bear left at a T-junction. Walk into Charlbury, retracing your outward steps back to the car park.

Walk B (7$^1/_4$ miles)

Route:
Follow Instructions 1 and 2 of Walk A to reach point 3 on the map.

Turn left. Walk along the road for $^1/4$ mile to a crossroads. Go straight over onto a road signposted to Leafield. This quiet country road with wide grass verges is shaded by trees for most of the way. In $^1/4$ mile turn right at a junction and continue on the road to Leafield. After a further $^1/2$ mile, opposite the entrance drive to Waterman's Lodge Farm, swing left over a stile onto a footpath through WYCHWOOD FOREST, signposted "Finstock 2". Now follow Instructions 7-10 of Walk A.

Points of Interest

CHARLBURY An attractive small town on high ground overlooking the Evenlode valley. The unspoilt centre has fine stone buildings, notably those lining Church Street where one row of houses hides behind a giant wisteria. At the lower end stands St Mary's church, mostly 13th to 15th century, but having a north arcade from Norman times.

SHORTHAMPTON Two or three cottages, a farm and a church comprise this remote hamlet. The church, a Norman foundation, retains an original font and window in the north wall. The window splay has what is probably the earliest mural decoration in the county - a pattern of roses enclosed by oblongs - dating from about 1200. Six other wall paintings, including Oxford's St Frideswide and the Miracle of the Clay Birds, originate from the 14th and 15th centuries. There are also fine Georgian box pews and a two-decker pulpit with its own wig stand.

WYCHWOOD FOREST The name "Wych" originates from "Hwicca" - a Saxon tribe who once controlled the region. Used as a royal hunting forest since Saxon times, Wychwood was extended by the Normans to cover about 70 square miles of Oxfordshire between Woodstock, Burford and Chipping Norton. In subsequent centuries it remained popular with royal hunters but gradually became fragmented and disafforested. Nowadays most of the remaining woodland (about 4 square miles) is confined to the Cornbury and Blenheim Estates.

CORNBURY PARK Once a hunting lodge within Wychwood Forest granted to royal favourites. Elizabeth I gave the house and park to Robert Dudley, Earl of Leicester, its most famous tenant. According to legend, the ghost of Dudley's wife (Amy Robsart), who died in 1560 under suspicious circumstances (see **Walk 18**), visited him in 1588 to warn of his imminent death. Within ten days he had sickened and passed away. The present house, largely a 17th century building, has a classical front. Now owned by Lord Rotherwick, the estate comprises a 600-acre deer park and part of Wychwood Forest.

WALK 11

Woodstock - Blenheim Park

(8 miles)

The 2,000 acres of magnificent parkland surrounding Blenheim Palace are the venue for this walk. Setting out from historic Woodstock the path follows public rights of way through the park via the Great Avenue and Akeman Street to reach the ancient hilltop village of Combe. Our return by leafy lakesides provides spectacular prospects of the palace and Grand Bridge.

O.S. Maps:	Landranger 164. Pathfinder 1092.
Start (447,168):	Hensington Road car park (with toilets), Woodstock. Approaching Woodstock from Oxford, turn right in the town centre and follow "Free Parking" signs. 8 miles NW of Oxford on the A44.
Terrain:	Mostly level: a few gentle inclines. Two stiles.
Refreshments:	Woodstock: a wide range available. Combe: The Cock Inn (Morrells) 01993-891288 G, CA in G, DA, food most days - phone to check. S.
Public Transport:	From Oxford: 20, 20A, B, C(T), X50(M) daily; 70(WO) M-Sat. From Witney: 42(T) M-Sat.

Route:

1.   From the car park, turn right and walk back into the centre of WOODSTOCK. Use a pedestrian crossing to reach the far side of the

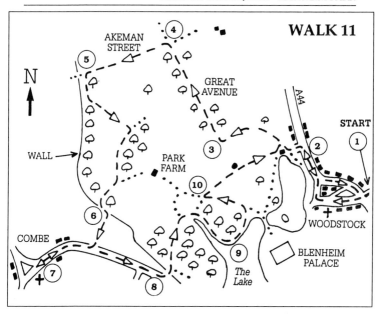

busy A44. Continue ahead on a path between buildings to enter a wide street with shops (High Street). Soon come to the imposing town hall - built of honey-brown Oxfordshire stone. Go forwards here into Park Street, passing the famous 13th century Bear Hotel on your left and five-legged stocks on the right. Our route takes us down Chaucers Lane, the final road on the right, but before going this way continue on Park Street, noting Chaucers House on your right and the majestic Triumphal Gate into Blenheim Palace, hidden round the corner. At the far end of Chaucers Lane take a flight of steps down Hoggrove Hill and re-enter the main road. Turn left. The roadside path at first descends and then climbs past houses and cottages.

2.   After 200 yards bear left at a footpath sign and enter the parkland of BLENHEIM PALACE via a small gate at the end of a short cul-de-sac. Follow a track downhill towards a lake (Queen Pool), at the same time enjoying your first view of the palace. The

track curves right to join a tarmac path. Continue along this path, with the lake on your left, to reach a cottage where the route forks. Proceed ahead along the bottom of a gently ascending, wooded valley. After crossing a cattle grid, the path veers first left, and then right, to enter the Great Avenue. Until the advent of Dutch Elm disease in the 1970s, a majestic avenue of mature elm trees stretched across this area of the park. Lime trees have now replaced the elms.

3.   Our route follows the Avenue for the next $^3/_4$ mile. Wide views open up in all directions, giving a wonderful feeling of spaciousness. The backward scene, towards the palace and Column of Victory, is especially notable. Ditchley Gate is straight ahead. On approaching Akeman Street, remnants of the ancient earthworks of GRIM'S DITCH (see **Walk 32**) are visible on both sides of the Avenue. At a fence and cattle grid, turn left onto the broad, grassy track of Akeman Street (part of the Oxfordshire Way, see **Appendix A**). Yellow arrows mark the route.

4.   After 100 yards pass through double gates into a field. A wood is on your right. When the wood comes to an end, carry on across an open area. Hares may be seen hereabouts, feeding or sprinting at speed across the fields. Ignore all side tracks and soon come to a belt of trees in a shallow valley. Halfway through the trees (30 yards short of the estate wall) swing left onto a farm track.

5.   In 200 yards turn left again. Cross a bridge over a stream and leave the trees. A grassy path ascends between open fields to reach a T-junction with a broad track running alongside a conifer plantation. Turn right. At the far end of the wood, where the track curves left to Park Farm, turn half right across an open field. Aim a few yards to the left of an electricity pole and towards the left-hand edge of the nearest clump of trees. Go round the edge of the trees. Follow a path along the field edge to the corner of the field. Our route turns right here to enter a wood before swinging left into an open valley. A diagonal path crosses the valley bottom and ascends between trees to a flight of steps over the estate wall.

6.   On the far side, turn left alongside the wall. In 200 yards pass through a gap in a hedge and bear right onto an uphill path following the field edge. Outlying buildings of Combe village are now visible on the horizon. When the hedge comes to an end, turn

half left across an open field to reach Park Road. Turn right and walk into the village of COMBE, an ideal picnic/refreshment stop.

7.   Retrace your steps along Park Road. The road runs along a ridge - offering splendid views across the Evenlode valley to the low wooded hills west of Oxford and the spire of Church Hanborough church. At a road junction, continue ahead past a post box and come to the Combe Lodge entrance to Blenheim Park.

8.   Enter through a side-gate into a lovely wooded area. Here, ancient oaks - remnants of Wychwood Forest - intermingle with younger trees while pheasants quietly forage in the undergrowth. After 100 yards turn left at a T-junction and follow the tarmac track downhill. In $^1/_3$ mile, where the route descends between cedar trees and veers left into a valley, branch right off the road onto a grassy track. This runs parallel to a fence along the valley bottom. Two hundred yards further on, cross a stile in the fence and turn right onto a delightful path beneath giant beech trees alongside a narrow lake. A rich variety of water birds frequent the area. The lake gradually widens and is soon revealed as no more than a creek of the vast Blenheim Lake.

9.   As the creek merges into the lake, our path climbs and swings left, opening up spectacular views across the lake to the Grand Bridge and palace. Continue uphill and in $^1/_4$ mile pass iron railings surrounding Fair Rosamund's Well - below trees on your right. A short distance further on, the path curves left to reach a T-junction with a metalled road. This is our closest approach to the palace. Bear left here and follow the road for $^1/_3$ mile until it dips into a hollow. On the left, a path runs away from the road down a shallow, wooded valley. Do not follow this path, but turn right.

10. Cross an open area and walk alongside a fence towards the Column of Victory. When the fence ends, continue straight ahead, passing the column on your left. Although no path is visible, our route curves a quarter right and goes downhill between two fenced plantations. As you descend, aim for a cottage at the left-hand end of a lake. Turn left at a tarmac track. In a short distance, swing sharply right to rejoin the outward route. Retrace your steps out of the park and back along the road to Woodstock. Do not go up the steps at Hoggrove Hill, but continue on the main road to arrive at

Hensington Road and the car park.

Points of Interest

WOODSTOCK Originally a clearing in Wychwood Forest where Henry I established a manor house and enclosed a park. The village of Woodstock grew up outside the park gates, becoming a market town in 1450. Today its finest thoroughfare (High Street/Park Street) leads to the Triumphal Gate and Blenheim Palace. Stone-built 16th to 18th century houses, mostly Georgian fronted, line the street giving it an air of solidity and prosperity. Notable buildings include: the Town Hall (1766); Fletcher's House - home of the County Museum; the church of St Mary Magdalene, largely rebuilt in 1878, but retaining a Norman doorway in the south aisle; Chaucer's House - named after the poet's son, a former owner of the manor.

BLENHEIM PALACE Conceived as a royal and national monument on a grand scale, Blenheim Palace is one of the finest 18th century buildings in Europe. It was erected in Woodstock Park for John Churchill, first Duke of Marlborough following his defeat of the French at the battle of Blenheim in 1704. Designed by Sir John Vanbrugh in the Baroque style, the palace is set in magnificent parkland landscaped by Capability Brown. A Great Avenue stretches for 2 miles across the park from the palace to Ditchley Gate; the arrangement of trees supposedly represents the disposition of troops at the battle of Blenheim. Within the Avenue, a statue of the Duke in Roman attire looks down from the Column of Victory. In 1874 another famous Churchill was born here, Sir Winston Churchill. (See **Appendix C** for opening times.)

COMBE A pub, a church, a shop and cottages of golden limestone surround a spacious village green. Originally a community beside the Evenlode, Combe was removed to its present hilltop location about 1350. Monks from Eynsham Abbey dismantled the riverside church and rebuilt it here in 1395. Inside is a rare stone pulpit with rich tracery; there are also fine 15th century stained glass windows and wall paintings. A Doom picture of Judgement Day over the chancel arch shows the condemned disappearing into the jaws of hell.

WALK 12

Bletchingdon - River Cherwell
(Walk A 5¹/₂ miles, Walk B 4 miles)

These two routes explore the lovely countryside north of Kidlington. They can be enjoyed separately or as a 9 mile "figure of eight" walk. Walk A gently ascends along field paths to the elevated village of Bletchingdon. Fine views are a feature of this walk. Heading north-west, Walk B soon reaches the haunting ruins of Hampton Gay Manor. It then joins the Oxford Canal towpath before meandering through lush Cherwell meadows back to Kidlington.

O.S. Maps:	Landranger 164. Pathfinder 1092.
Start (497,148):	Park and start at St Mary's church, Kidlington. 5 miles N of Oxford on the A4260. From Oxford turn right at traffic lights in the Kidlington shopping area (signposted: Oxfordshire Fire Service HQ). Follow the road into the High Street. Go to the end. Continue ahead to the far end of Church Street.
Terrain:	Walk A: Gentle inclines. Four stiles. Walk B: Mostly level. Twenty-two stiles.
Refreshments:	Hampton Poyle: The Gonefish Inn (Free House) 01865 373926 SDA, G, PA, CA, DA. Bletchingdon: The Blacks Head (Pubmaster) 01869-350315 G, CA in G, DA. S. Thrupp: The Boat Inn (Morrells) 01865-374279 SDA, CA, G, DA in G.
Public Transport:	From Oxford: 2/2A(O/CL) daily. Alight at the High Street and follow the instructions for drivers, above.

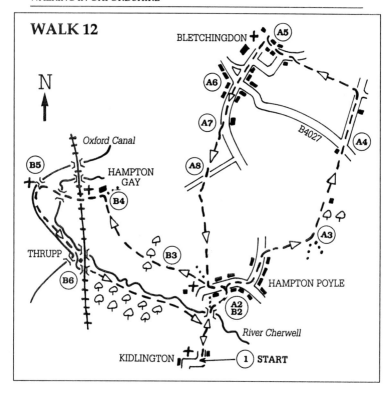

WALK 12

N

Oxford Canal

BLETCHINGDON

HAMPTON GAY

THRUPP

HAMPTON POYLE

River Cherwell

KIDLINGTON

① START

B4027

Walk A (5¹/₂ miles)

Route:

A1. Before leaving KIDLINGTON note some interesting almshouses beside the church. Cross a stile (no signpost) next to a car park at the rear of the church. Follow the path straight ahead for ¹/₄ mile, first over scrub land and then alongside a meadow to reach a concrete bridge over the River Cherwell. Cross to a field on the other side. Turn a quarter right and walk towards a wide gap in the opposite hedge, filled by wooden fencing and 80 yards right of the far left-hand field corner. Climb a stile in the fencing. Follow a track around a field and past gardens to arrive at a T-junction with

74

Church Lane in the village of Hampton Poyle.

A2.   Turn right. Our route continues along this quiet lane for 200 yards past a variety of attractive, stone-built houses to reach a junction. Turn left. When the houses come to an end, branch right onto a gravelled farm track labelled with a "No bridleway" sign. After 30 yards climb a locked metal gate. The track proceeds along the edge of four fields for $^{1}/_{2}$ mile. Look left from the final field to see outlying houses of Bletchingdon and the white chimney of Shipton cement works. At the field end, our track passes between a pair of old wooden gateposts before veering right. A white disc is attached to the back of the left-hand post.

A3.   Turn left here onto a grassy bridleway following the left-hand edge of a field. Proceed through a gap in the far hedge and across a second field, passing the quaintly named Frogsnest Farm, with its derelict wind pump, on the way. An opening through the next hedge, beside Diamond Farm (ice cream here in summer), brings us to the B4027 road.

A4.   Proceed ahead on a quiet lane, signposted to Weston-on-the-Green. After $^{1}/_{3}$ mile swing left along a footpath to Bletchingdon. Our path follows the edge of the first field and ascends straight across the second. From the top of the latter, look back for a good view across Otmoor, with Beckley TV mast on the horizon. Walk through a small woodland to enter a metalled road in BLETCHINGDON. Turn left. In 100 yards, when the road veers left, continue forwards on a tarmac drive. Soon reach a junction of paths beside the church. The building is kept locked but the key can be obtained from the rector. Turn right. Walk past the refurbished stable block of Bletchingdon Park to a stile on the far side and enjoy distant views to the north-east.

A5.   Retrace your steps to the church. Proceed forwards on a shaded path past the impressive edifice of Bletchingdon Park to arrive at a road. Continue ahead on a roadside path, with delightful stone-built houses on your left and the boundary wall of Bletchingdon Park on the right. Soon arrive at a triangular village green.

A6.   Keep going in the same direction past the green, over crossroads, and along the road to Hampton Poyle. Three hundred yards beyond the last house in Bletchingdon, come to Village Farm on your left. Go past the first farm entrance. Opposite the second, walk through a metal gate into a field and swing left.

A7. Follow the field edge past a solitary oak (remnants of a waymark attached) to reach the corner. Proceed through a metal gate into a second field. Fine views over the Cherwell valley can be enjoyed from this point. Turn half right and walk diagonally across the field. Aim for a point on the field boundary to the right of Kidlington church spire and 100 yards short of the far right-hand corner. Climb a stile through the hedge into a third field. Turn half left and cross the field, aiming for the right-hand side of one of the largest trees on the far boundary. Pass through the trees and over a narrow, metalled road.

A8. Bear half right to follow a path across the next field. Our route now crosses three more fields before reaching a double stile close to Hampton Poyle church. If the path is not visible across the first field, walk straight ahead, aiming for the second tree left of Kidlington church spire; on entering the second field, turn half right and go towards the spire-like radio mast of Thames Valley Police Headquarters in Kidlington; at the third field, aim directly at Kidlington church spire. Finally cross the double stile and a narrow field to enter a metalled lane in Hampton Poyle. (If you are on the 9 mile walk, do not cross the double stile but turn round at this point and follow Instruction B2 from sentence four.) Turn left. In 300 yards swing right beside cottages and retrace the outward route back to Kidlington.

Walk B (4 miles)

Route:
This walk follows part of the Kidlington Circular Walk, so look out for CR (Circular Route) markers. Follow Instruction 1 of Walk A to reach point A2/B2 on the map. Now continue.

B2. Turn left. In 300 yards bear right over a stile immediately before Hampton Poyle church. Take a signposted path across a narrow meadow, climb a double stile and swing left. Follow the left-hand field edge. After 25 yards the track goes left through a hedge and over another double stile to reach a field. Here, a vast hedged pasture has been subdivided by fences to accommodate horses. Our objective is to reach the far right-hand corner of the original field. Turn half right and aim for the most distant of two metal gates in the same fence. A white disc is attached to the gate post. Climb the gate and turn three-quarters left. Cross a small field to a stile 20 yards from the near left-hand corner. Beyond the stile, turn half right and walk towards the far right-hand corner of the original field.

B3. The route now crosses four more fields on its way to Hampton Gay. Normally our track is clearly visible across the first three of these fields. If this is not the case, the directions to be taken at the start of each field are as follows: turn a quarter right, downhill to a line of trees; turn a quarter left, uphill; straight ahead. From the third field enjoy a panoramic view which includes: Oxford Airport, the white chimney of Shipton cement works, and the churches of Hampton Gay and Shipton. Keep to the left edge of the fourth field until it veers left. At this point, turn half right and strike out across the field towards the left end of a splendid row of horse chestnuts, partially hiding the ruins of Hampton Gay Manor. Undulations in the field indicate where the houses of HAMPTON GAY once stood.

B4. Turn left at a route marker beneath the left-hand tree and walk towards the lonely church of St Giles - normally open (key from Manor Farm, if closed). A noticeboard outside recounts the village story. On leaving the church, bear a quarter right and walk to a white stile next to the railway. Cross the track. Proceed ahead to a wooden electricity pole in a field. Turn half right. Aim for a gap between trees to reach a footbridge over the Cherwell. Our path continues across the next field and along a farm track to a bridge over the OXFORD CANAL (**Walk 1** and **Appendix A**). Do not cross the bridge, but swing left along the towpath.

B5. For the next ¹/₂ mile we follow the canal to Thrupp - a tiny hamlet built for bargemen with a basin and wharf, now used to service pleasure boats. For much of the way colourful narrow boats line the bank, with the Cherwell keeping us company on the left. At Thrupp the path turns right to a swing bridge (Aubrey's Bridge).

B6. To visit the hamlet, cross the bridge and bear left; otherwise turn left through Thrupp Maintenance Yard. Go forwards past the right-hand side of thatched cottages and under a railway bridge to enter Thrupp Community Woodland. Thousands of trees have been planted in the water-meadows and a network of permissive paths created to improve public access. Take a path beside the river. For the next mile delight in an idyllic stretch of the meandering Cherwell - hidden in places by pollarded willows, reeds, rushes and tall grasses. In summertime, yellow water lilies and white water crowfoot adorn the surface while mallard, moorhen, swan and coot feed contentedly in the peace and solitude of this part of the river. Finally arrive at the concrete bridge crossed on our outward journey. Bear right here and retrace your steps back to Kidlington.

Points of Interest

KIDLINGTON St Mary's church, originally built by the Abbot of Osney in the 13th century, gained a 170ft (52m) spire some 200 years later. It is now a prominent feature of the local landscape. Alongside the church stand grey stone almshouses given to the village in 1671 by Sir William Morton, a local landowner and judge. Lintels above the windows bear the names of his children.

BLETCHINGDON Houses of local limestone partially surround a pleasant, tree-lined green beside the walls of Bletchingdon Park. A Palladian style house in the park, built for the Earl of Anglesey in 1782, was extensively refurbished in 1995. A previous house on the same site had been an important Royalist stronghold during the Civil War. In 1645 it was besieged by Cromwell. After pleas from his frightened wife, the young Royalist commander, Colonel Windebank, surrendered the house to the Roundheads. Following an exchange of prisoners, he was court-martialled and shot.

HAMPTON GAY Nowadays all that remains of a once properous village is the little church of St Giles, a ruined Elizabethan manor house, a farm and a few cottages. During the 18th and early 19th centuries a community of 86 souls flourished here, the church being rebuilt in 1767. However, the end of the 1800s brought disaster and ruin to Hampton Gay. On Christmas Eve, 1874, part of a London to Birmingham train left the track near to the village and crashed into the River Cherwell. Thirty-four people died and over one hundred were injured. It was the worst railway accident to date. Thirteen years later, the local paper mill closed and the manor house was burnt down, leaving most villagers unemployed. Hampton Gay never recovered.

WALK 13

Piddington - Muswell Hill

(4³/₄ miles)

Straddling the Oxfordshire-Buckinghamshire border, Muswell Hill commands superb panoramas over both counties. From the pretty village of Piddington our walk gradually climbs to the summit along attractive field paths, on the way passing through a rich variety of trees and flowers in Piddington Wood.

O.S. Maps:	Landranger 164 or 165. Pathfinder 1093.
Start (640,170):	Park and start at Piddington church. 5 miles SE of Bicester on a minor road off the A41.
Terrain:	A gradual climb followed by a quick descent. Fifteen stiles.
Public Transport:	From Oxford and/or Bicester: 94(CO) M-Sat, 3(CO) F. To Widnell Lane, ¹/₂ mile from Point 2 on the walk: 29(T, GL) M-Sat, 27(T) Sun, Public Hols.

Route:

1.   From the church, walk northwards into PIDDINGTON village. Twenty-five yards before reaching the pub, turn left at a wooden footpath sign. The path goes through a gap in a hedge and straight ahead across an open field. Aim for a wooden electricity pole in the middle. At the far side, pass through a metal gate and follow a curved track to the distant right-hand corner of the next field.

2.   From now on, most of the route follows Circular Walk signs. Do not cross the stile at this point, but turn sharply left onto a path running along the field edge. Muswell Hill, crowned with tall trees, can be seen on the skyline ahead. Climb a stile at the field end. Our

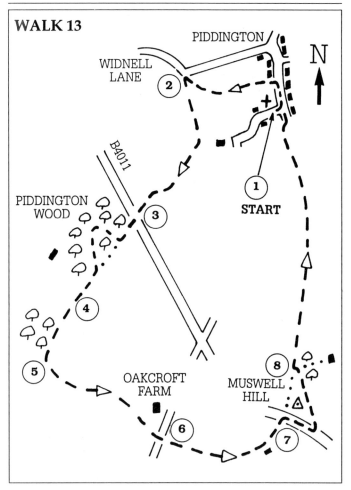

WALK 13

PIDDINGTON

WIDNELL
LANE

②

N

B4011

PIDDINGTON
WOOD

③

④

⑤

OAKCROFT
FARM

⑥

①

START

⑧

MUSWELL
HILL

⑦

walk continues along the right-hand edge of two more fields,
passing Hill Farm on the left and crossing another stile before
reaching a gate. Beyond the gate, walk diagonally across the next
field to a second gate in the distant right-hand corner. Go through

and turn right. Follow a field edge to the corner. Swing left here and proceed uphill alongside a derelict barbed wire fence to arrive at the B4011.

3.   Cross the road and enter Piddington Wood. After 200 yards turn right off the main track onto a path descending into the depths of the wood. Besides enjoying the trees, birds and flowers, you may also catch a glimpse of a fox or muntjac deer. In a further 200 yards arrive at a clearing. Turn left and walk uphill to reach the main track. Turn right. Climb a stile at the end of the wood and swing right.

4.   Follow a path around the field edge. Bullingdon Prison, screened by poplar trees, and the huge ordnance depot on Arncott Hill can be seen on your right. Continue for ¹/₄ mile to the field corner before turning left.

5.   For the next 1¹/₄ miles our route follows the Oxfordshire-Buckinghamshire border to the top of MUSWELL HILL. Initially the track (now a bridleway) runs alongside a double barbed wire fence enclosing hawthorn bushes before going through a gate into the next field. Keep to the right-hand edge of three more fields, passing Oakcroft Farm on the way, to reach a road.

6.   Cross to the far side and follow a bridleway ascending the left-hand edge of a field. At the top, go through a wooden gate. Our track now climbs for ¹/₂ mile along the right-hand edge of the next field. Look back occasionally for an ever widening view of Oxfordshire. On approaching the summit, pass through a steel gate into a road. Turn right.

7.   Proceed along the road, enjoying good views over Buckinghamshire, with the village of Oakley nestling in the valley to your right. After 400 yards climb a stile through the hedge on your left. Bear half left and take a path passing near to the triangulation point. Superb panoramas open up from this field. Beyond a stile at the field end note some square earthworks (The Wilderness), about 70 yards across and 2 yards high, beneath trees on your right. Turn left and walk along the entrance drive of Muswell Hill Farm. In 40 yards go through a small wooden gate on the right.

8.   Turn right. Take a track along the edge of a field which falls away to the left, giving spectacular views over Oxfordshire. As the

path descends, Piddington comes into view straight ahead. The route continues along field edges and wide tracks as it crosses two single and two double stiles. After the second double stile, turn a quarter left. Walk across an open field, aiming for a large house with four attic windows and a red tiled roof. At the far side go through a gate into the next field. Turn three-quarters right. Go towards a stile situated between two buildings; the path runs parallel to the right-hand field edge. Cross the stile and in 40 yards enter a lane. Turn left to reach the starting point, a short distance away.

Points of Interest

PIDDINGTON A quiet border settlement extending for $1^1/4$ miles along a winding lane. A stream next to the lane once served as the village water supply. At the southern end stands the 13th century church of St Nicholas. Its original chancel is lit by colourful Victorian glass set in beautiful triple lancet windows, while a faint 14th century painting of St Christopher, uncovered in 1933, decorates the north wall of the nave. In the churchyard lies the poet John Drinkwater (1882-1937), who spent part of his boyhood at the manor.

MUSWELL HILL 650ft, 198m. The origin of square earthworks (The Wilderness) near to the summit is uncertain. Being commanded by higher ground to the south, they are unlikely to have been a Roman camp but may have enclosed a hedge maze - "wilderness" being a medieval term for such a feature. Ordnance depots on Arncott Hill (2 miles NE) and wooded Graven Hill ($4^1/2$ miles NE) can be seen from here. Deliberately built on hills (in 1942) to make bombing difficult, they continue to provide supplies for the army.

WALK 14

OTMOOR: ISLIP AND BECKLEY
(Walk A 8 miles, Walk B 5 miles)

The primeval fenland of Otmoor is a wonderful haven for wildlife and a magical place to visit. Setting out from historic Islip we soon enjoy some fine views across the moor. The longer route continues to the hilltop village of Beckley before crossing wide expanses of fenland; the shorter route returns along a tranquil section of the River Cherwell.

O.S. Maps:	Landranger 164. Pathfinder 1092.
Start (528,139):	Islip public car park, by the river bridge, and opposite The Swan pub. 5 miles N of Oxford on the B4027.
Terrain:	Level or gentle inclines. Walk A: seventeen stiles. Walk B: eleven stiles.
Refreshments:	Islip: The Red Lion (Greenalls) 01865-375367 SDA, G (April-Sept), PA, CA in SDA if over the age of 10, DA in G, no food Sun and M evenings Sept-April. S. Beckley: Abingdon Arms (Free House) 01865-351311 G, CA in G, DA on lead, no food Sun evening.
Public Transport:	Rail: Oxford-Bicester (TT) M-Sat. Bus: Oxford-Bicester 94(CO) M-Sat; Oxford-Murcott 95(CO) W, F.

Walk A (8 miles)

Route:

1.	For the first 3¹/₂ miles we follow the Oxfordshire Way (**Appendix A**). From the car park cross a bridge over the River Ray and take a roadside path climbing out of ISLIP. Twenty yards past speed restriction signs, turn left through a metal gate onto a concrete drive. In a further 25 yards veer right onto a farm track and cross a stile into a field. Our route now continues in the same direction across four fields. Extensive views open up over OTMOOR to Muswell Hill (the highest of the surrounding hills), Brill Hill (right of Muswell Hill), and the lower summits of Graven Hill (wooded) and Arncott Hill. Look back for a panoramic view over Islip and the Oxfordshire Plain. On entering the fifth field, bear a quarter left. Aim for a group of bushes on the horizon to the left of Beckley TV transmission mast. Cross a stile and follow a path through the bushes. After 200 yards enter a metalled lane in the village of NOKE. Turn left.

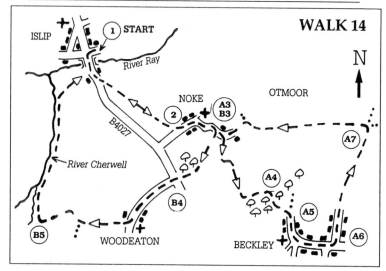

2. Soon arrive at the church (open). Proceed for a further ¹/₂ mile along a road which twists and turns its way through this quiet backwater. Ignore a footpath to Woodeaton part way through the village. On reaching the end of Noke (just before the road veers left) note a signposted bridleway to Woodeaton on your right.

A3. Continue along the road for a further 100 yards. Turn right onto a signposted path following the right-hand edge of a vast field. After ³/₄ mile the track swings left beside Noke Wood - a plantation which contains remnants of the medieval Forest of Shotover. Look left here to see the splendid battlemented tower of Charlton-on-Otmoor church and the less distinct Oddington church tower, with its pyramid-shaped roof, some 2¹/₂ miles away across the moor. In a further ¹/₄ mile enter Noke Wood.

A4. A short path quickly brings us to scrub on the far side. Veer right between bushes and follow a rising gradient alongside a fence. After 100 yards the track turns left over a stile. Head diagonally uphill across a field and climb a stile 100 yards left of the distant corner. The path continues in the same direction to the far right-hand corner of a second field. Look back from here for a magnificent panorama of Otmoor.

A5.   Climb a stile. Turn right into a lane leading uphill into the picturesque village of BECKLEY. Bear left at a T-junction beside the church (open) and walk down the High Street past the Abingdon Arms. When the main road veers right, continue forwards. In 100 yards branch left down Otmoor Lane - a lane following the course of a Roman road which once crossed the moor on its way from Dorchester-on-Thames to Alchester, a Roman town $1^1/_2$ miles south of Bicester.

A6.   This quiet lane gradually descends onto the moor. Three hundred yards beyond the drive to Lower Farm, pass the entrance to Otmoor Range, a Ministry of Defence rifle range. Continue ahead. In 150 yards the metalled lane becomes a grassy track. After a further $^1/_4$ mile come to a wooden gate across the track, marking the rifle range boundary. Turn left.

A7.   Walk along a causeway with drainage ditches on either side. The vast expanse of uncultivated moor stretching away to the right allows one to envisage how the original fenland might have looked. Gaps in the hedge on your left allow good views of Beckley. After $1^1/_4$ miles swing left over a wide concrete bridge onto a farm track. In 300 yards pass the buildings of Lower Farm and come to a metalled lane. Turn right. Follow the lane into Noke and retrace your outward journey across the fields back to Islip.

Walk B (5 miles)

Route:
Follow Instructions 1 and 2 of Walk A to reach point A3/B3 on the map. Now continue from Instruction B3.

B3.   Turn right along the bridleway to Woodeaton. After $^1/_3$ mile the track passes through the edge of Prattle Wood. In springtime, bluebells transform the woodland floor from dull brown to a brilliant azure. Beyond the wood our path soon reaches the B4027 road.

B4.   Cross to the far side and take a single track road to Woodeaton. In $^1/_2$ mile arrive at the village green with its ancient preaching cross. Inside the church is a huge wall painting of St Christopher. On leaving the church return to the back of the churchyard. Cross over the road. Slip through a narrow gap beside a metal gate onto a footpath signposted: "Cutteslow 2$^{1}/_{4}$". Our route now follows a farm track for $^{1}/_{2}$ mile to a point where it divides. Take the right fork alongside a dry-stone wall. The prominent white building across fields on your left is the John Radcliffe Hospital, 3 miles distant in Oxford. In a further 200 yards the left hedgerow comes to an end. Turn left here. Follow a path along the field edge to the corner. Turn right.

B5.   The path continues along the field edge, with a stream on your left. Beyond a field on the far bank stand the impressive 17th century buildings of Water Eaton Manor. The stream soon joins the Cherwell. For the next $^{2}/_{3}$ mile our route keeps to the tree-lined river bank, crossing two more stiles on the way. Eventually, the tower of Islip church and spire of Kidlington church come into view. Turn right alongside a wire fence at the next field boundary. In 100 yards veer left over a stile and turn half right across an open field. Cross a stile on the far side. The path proceeds along the left-hand side of the next field before passing allotments and going between cottages to reach a main road in Islip. Turn left here and retrace your steps to the car park.

Points of Interest

ISLIP Since the days of Saxon kings, Islip has had connections with royalty. In about 1004 a royal palace north of the village saw the birth of Edward the Confessor, builder of Westminster Abbey; in his will he left "ye little town of Islippe" to the abbey. Westminster still appoints rectors of Islip. A portrait of Edward together with an extract from his will are kept in the church.

The village grew up around a ford across the River Ray near to its confluence with the Cherwell. The bridge which eventually replaced the ford became the scene of several skirmishes during the Civil War as both sides sought to control this strategic river crossing. Later, the London-Worcester turnpike used the same bridge. For centuries, Islip was famed for its eels - caught with osier cages in the River Ray.

OTMOOR Often hidden by autumn mists, this mysterious wilderness has proved difficult to drain and convert to arable farming. From time immemorial local villagers have had the right to graze animals on the moor, to fish and to take wildfowl. In 1830 attempts to enclose the fenland met with stout opposition; new fences, hedges, embankments, gates and bridges were all smashed down. Since that time, part of the fen has been lost to agriculture but much remains as wetland.

Ironically, use of the moor as a bombing range during the Second World War and current use of the central area as a rifle range have helped to preserve it as a wilderness. Today the central area is a Site of Special Scientific Interest and home to a huge variety of birds, butterflies, insects and plants, including several rare species.

Otmoor has proved to be an inspiration for many writers. The idea of including a giant chessboard in *Through the Looking Glass* is reputed to have come to Lewis Carroll as he looked down at the pattern of fields across the moor.

NOKE One of the seven "towns" of Otmoor, whose name means "by the oak trees". The present 13th century church of St Giles contains an earlier font given by Princess Gundreda, Lady of the Manor of Noke and youngest daughter of William the Conqueror. An old piece of doggerel refers to the villagers and those in neighbouring Beckley:

> "I went to Noke and nobody spoke,
> I went to Beckley and they spoke directly."

BECKLEY An unspoilt village of stone-built cottages in a high position overlooking Otmoor. The well-kept, spacious church, mostly 14th century, holds some treasures worthy of inspection: a fascinating set of 14th century wall paintings, rare windows of a similar age in the north aisle, one of the oldest parish chests (1250) in the country, a Jacobean pulpit and a Norman tub font.

WALK 15
Burford - Windrush Valley
(Walk A 6¹/₄ miles, Walk B 5 miles, Walk C 4 miles)

A ramble through an idyllic part of the Windrush valley in the Oxfordshire Cotswolds. Leaving the impressive wool town of Burford our route follows lane, field path and water-meadow to visit the pretty riverside villages of Widford, Swinbrook and Asthall. Allow extra time to explore Burford - a most rewarding experience.

O.S. Maps:	Landranger 163. Pathfinder 1091.
Start (254,123):	Free car park, Church Lane, Burford. 7 miles W of Witney on the A40 and A361.
Terrain:	Gentle inclines and one moderate climb. Walk A: fifteen stiles. Walk B: ten stiles. Walk C: nine stiles.
Refreshments:	Burford: a wide range available. Swinbrook: The Swan (Free House) 01993-822165 M-Sat 12-1.30, 6.30-8.45, Sun 12-1.30. This is a tiny pub; please phone beforehand if your party exceeds eight. Asthall: The Maytime (Free House) 01993-822068 SDA, G, CA, CM, DA, daily 11-3, 6-11.
Public Transport:	From Oxford and Witney 53(S) daily, X3(T) M-Sat.

Walk A (6¹/₄ miles)

Route:

1.   From the car park walk back along Church Lane to BURFORD High Street. Turn right. Cross a bridge over the Windrush and turn right again at a mini-roundabout. In 300 yards reach the edge of Fulbrook village. Pause for a moment at a stone seat next to the path and look right for a good view of Burford. Soon pass the end of Walnut Row. Twenty yards further on, turn right onto a narrow path beside Cotland House. The route goes across two stiles before veering left through a narrow paddock and kissing gate onto a

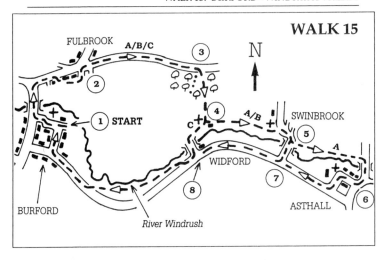

WALK 15

fenced path. In 150 yards cross a stile and follow the left-hand edge of a field to the far end. Bear left over a stile. Follow a track between gardens to reach a lane. Turn right. Walk between stone cottages to the centre of Fulbrook and swing right at the war memorial. After 100 yards, branch half right onto a single track road to Swinbrook.

2. This quiet road, with wide grassy verges, gradually climbs out of Fulbrook village. A well positioned seat near to the summit offers splendid views of Burford and the Cotswold Hills. At the summit itself look right for a distant prospect of the White Horse Hill and North Wessex Downs, some 20 miles away. Three-quarters of a mile beyond Fulbrook the road dips sharply at the far end of a wood. Turn right here over a stile ("only to Widford and Swinbrook"). Do not take a bridleway 30 yards earlier.

3. Our track now descends into the Windrush valley along the floor of a shallow grassy coomb (Dean Bottom). At the far end go through a gate into a field. Continue downhill in the same direction to reach a farm track. Turn right. Walk along the track and over a cattle grid set within a dry-stone wall. Immediately turn right. Climb across the field to WIDFORD church - a solitary place encapsulating 2,000 years of English history. The door latch is rather

stiff so press hard! On leaving the church, retrace your steps to the farm track.

4.   Turn left and return over the cattle grid. Walk straight ahead across the field traversed previously, aiming for a wooden post left of a farmhouse garden. At the far side our route passes through a gap in a stone wall and then crosses two delightful meadows - speckled with golden buttercups in summertime. At the end of the second meadow go through a gate into a walled path which soon becomes a cobbled lane leading to the village of SWINBROOK. (To visit the church, a diversion can be made via a small white gate on the left.) In 100 yards reach a T-junction with a metalled road. Bear right and walk gently downhill through this scattered village to arrive at The Swan Inn.

5.   Turn left here over a stone stile onto a path signposted to Asthall. The path proceeds over a meadow and a pair of stiles before splitting into two. Take the right fork towards the river. Follow the river bank to a stile in the far hedge and cross another meadow before coming to a metalled road. Turn right. Go over a bridge and soon enter the charming village of ASTHALL.

6.   At the village centre swing right past the Maytime Inn towards the church and manor house. At the church, bear left to reach a T-junction. Turn right. In 50 yards look through a stone arch for a good view of Asthall Manor. For much of the way our return route follows a quiet road back to Burford. After $1/2$ mile go ahead over crossroads.

7.   Pass a recreation ground and in a further $1/2$ mile arrive at the hamlet of Widford. Continue in the same direction, ignoring a side-road to Widford church.

8.   Two hundred yards beyond Widford, the road veers a quarter left. Go forwards here over a stile beside a metal gate, labelled "Private Fishing Cotswold Fly Fishers". For the next $3/4$ mile, we follow a tranquil riverside path before re-entering the road. Turn right. Soon join a roadside path, lined with lime trees, leading into Burford. Opposite The Royal Oak pub, bear right into Guildenford and quickly reach the starting point in Church Lane.

Swinbrook

Walk B (5 miles)

Route:

Follow Instructions 1 to 4 of Walk A, to reach point 5 on the map. Continue along the road. Cross Swinbrook bridge and in 200 yards come to a crossroads. Turn right. Now follow Walk A from Instruction 7.

Walk C (4 miles)

Route:

Follow Instructions 1 to 3 of Walk A to reach point 4 on the map. Bear right along the farm track. In 250 yards cross a cattle grid and enter a metalled lane. Turn left. Cross a bridge over the Windrush and come to a T-junction in the hamlet of Widford. Turn right. Now follow Walk A from Instruction 8.

Points of Interest

BURFORD A beautiful Cotswold town whose charm lies in the harmony of its golden stone buildings and a spectacular vista down the High Street. During medieval times, the wool trade, coaching inns and saddlery brought prosperity to the town, many of its buildings dating from this period.

Besides enjoying the High Street and streets visited during the walk, take a look at Sheep Street and Priory Lane. The Priory (in Priory Lane), a 12th century Augustinian foundation, was at one time owned by William Lenthall, Speaker of the Long Parliament. In recent years it has reverted to its original use. The town museum is housed in 16th century Tolsey House - a place where market tolls were once collected.

The church, second largest in Oxfordshire, boasts a magnificent spire and fine monuments to the Harmon and Tanfield families. Bale wool tombs in the churchyard testify to an earlier source of wealth. An inscription "Anthony Sedley prisner 1649" on the font is a reminder that during the Civil War four hundred mutineers of the Parliamentary Army were rounded up in the district and imprisoned in the church. Cromwell had the three ringleaders shot; a small plaque on the outside of the church wall, left of the door, is their memorial.

WIDFORD Undulations in fields around the church are all that remains of the deserted medieval village of Widford. Its 13 households in 1381 had dwindled to a mere three by 1524. Thirteenth century St Oswald's is built on the site of a Roman villa whose mosaic pavement forms part of the chancel floor. Prior to restoration, the mosaic has been covered to prevent it from becoming "an irresistible quarry to some of our visitors"! There are also interesting 14th century murals and 19th century box pews. Three hundred yards away on the Windrush stands a 16th century manor house with mullioned windows.

SWINBROOK A delightful village scattered along the Wenrisc stream - a tributary of the Windrush. Amazing 17th century monuments of the Fettiplace family - six reclining noblemen in two triple tiers - cover a chancel wall in St Mary's church. In the churchyard, just west of the church porch, are the graves of Nancy Mitford, 20th century novelist, and one of her sisters, Unity.

ASTHALL Originally a Roman settlement on Akeman Street - the road from St Albans to Cirencester. The only proven Roman Camp in Oxfordshire (identified by crop marks in 1994) lies $1/3$ mile SW of the village. A unique stone altar and a 14th century effigy of Lady Joan Cornwall, wife of Edmund Cornwall (grandson of King John) and one time owner of the village, can be seen in the church. Behind the church stands a Jacobean manor, built in 1620 and from 1919 to 1926 home to the Mitford family, including the six well-known sisters.

WALK 16
Witney - Minster Lovell
(5 miles)

The romantic ruins of Minster Lovell Hall, set beside an idly flowing Windrush, form the focal point of this walk. Starting from the edge of Witney our route snakes through fields and woodland of the Windrush valley to reach the quiet Cotswold village of Minster Lovell. The return path takes a similar route on the far side of the valley.

O.S. Maps:	Landranger 164. Pathfinder 1091.
Start (347,103):	Park and start at a lay-by opposite The Windrush Inn, Burford Road (A4095), Witney.
Terrain:	Level and gentle inclines. Sixteen stiles.
Refreshments:	Witney: The Windrush (Courage) 01993-702612 SDA, G, CA, CM, DA, M-Sat 11 am-12 pm, Sun 12-3, 7-10.30. Minster Lovell: The Old Swan (Style Conferences) 01993-774441 SDA, G, CA, DA in G, M-F 11-3, 6-11, Sat, Sun all day. Crawley: The Lamb Inn (Free House) 01993-703753 G, CA, PA, DA in G, M-F 12-3, 6-11, Sat 12-11, Sun 12-10.30.
Public Transport:	From Oxford: 100(T) daily; 109(O/CL) M-Sat. Alight in Corn Street. Walk away from the town centre to reach a roundabout. Bear right up Tower Hill. At the end, turn left and follow Route Instruction 1 from sentence three.

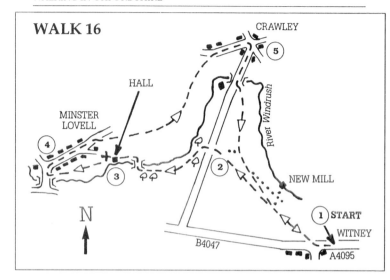

WALK 16

Route:

1. Before or after the walk you may wish to explore the historic centre of WITNEY. From the lay-by, cross over the road and turn left towards a garage. Twenty yards beyond a mini-roundabout, bear right onto a signposted bridleway ("Minster Lovell 2"), gradually descending into the Windrush valley. In ⅓ mile pass through a metal gate. Continue forwards for 50 yards before turning half left over a stile onto an uphill path crossing a field. Crawley village lies on the far side of the valley, beyond the tall chimneys of Crawley Mill. Look back from here for a good view of the meandering Windrush. Our path exits the field via a gap in a hedge.

2. Proceed ahead across a road, two stiles and a narrow field before descending through a wood of coppiced hazel (Maggots Grove). Leave the wood by another stile. The path now traverses five meadows before entering coniferous woodland. One hundred and fifty yards into the trees, veer right towards the Windrush. Follow the river bank to a wooden footbridge and cross to a meadow on the far side. The ruins of Minster Lovell Hall can be seen

ahead. Pollarded willows, a common feature of the Windrush valley, are especially prominent in this area. Soon pass through the kissing gate entrance to MINSTER LOVELL Hall.

3.   After viewing the ruins, take a path beside the entrance kiosk leading into a churchyard. Once inside, turn right to visit the church, otherwise go forwards to a gate on the far side. The track now crosses two meadows before reaching a recreation ground; aim for a gate, 50 yards left of the cricket pavilion. Walk through the gate and swing right onto a roadside path. After 100 yards turn right into the pretty village street of Minster Lovell, lined with Cotswold stone cottages.

4.   In $1/4$ mile pass a side road leading to Minster Lovell church; 300 yards further on turn right onto a path signposted to Crawley. Our route now goes across two fields before proceeding uphill on a wide, grassy path. There is a good view of Crawley from the top of the incline. After crossing a stile the path becomes a farm track which eventually reaches a metalled road. Turn right here and descend into Crawley village.

5.   Bear right at the war memorial and keep to a footpath alongside the main road. One hundred yards beyond a bridge over the Windrush, turn left onto a bridleway. In $1/3$ mile pass through two metal gates. Note the buildings of New Mill across a field on your left. When the path divides, take the right fork following an upward gradient between hawthorn bushes. After $1/4$ mile rejoin the outward route and retrace your steps back to Witney.

Points of Interest

WITNEY In spite of modern developments Witney retains some fine buildings from earlier days. Pride of place goes to the unusual Buttercross (1660) - a pavilion supported by 13 pillars once used as a covered market. The open arches of a simple Town Hall and Victorian Corn Exchange stand opposite. In the other direction, Tudor, Georgian and Victorian buildings enclose a broad, tree-lined green, dominated at the far end by the magnificent church of St Mary with its soaring spire. Fronting onto the High Street and boasting a fine single-handed clock is the Blanket Weavers' Hall (1721). At one time every Witney blanket was weighed and measured

95

here before dispatch around the world. It is a reminder of Witney's fame as a centre for blanket manufacture - an activity which continues to this day.

MINSTER LOVELL A name originating from the church (or minster) and the Lovell family - lords of the manor from the 12th to 15th centuries. Minster Lovell Hall and church were built in the early 15th century by William, 7th Lord Lovell. Before being dismantled in 1747, the Hall - one of the outstanding houses of Oxfordshire - enclosed three sides of a quadrangle, the fourth remaining open to the river.

An intriguing mystery surrounds the fate of Francis, the ninth and last Lord Lovell. After fighting for the losing side at the battle of Stoke (1487) he was last seen fleeing across the River Trent. According to legend he made his way back to Minster Lovell where a servant secretly hid him in a locked, underground room. When the servant died, Francis was left to expire. In 1708 this story gained some credibility when a new chimney was being installed and "there was discovered a large vault or room underground, in which was the entire skeleton of a man, as having been sitting at a table, which was before him, with a book, paper, pen, etc."

WALK 17

Shotover - Wheatley
(Walk A 6¹/₂ miles, Walk B 3 miles)

Setting out from suburban Oxford we quickly cross the Eastern Bypass and plunge into Shotover Country Park - a wondrous world of trees, birds and flowers. The walk continues to the top of Shotover Hill, offering fine views across the county, before dropping down through the grounds of Shotover House to the village of Wheatley. The return leg follows the old stagecoach route from London.

O.S. Maps:	Landranger 164. Pathfinder 1116.
Start (553,059):	Park and start at Wood Farm shops, Atkyns Road. Turn off the Eastern Bypass (A4142) at

The Great Coxwell tithe barn (Walk 24)
View from the Thames Path between Culham and Abingdon
(Walk 25)

Brightwell Barrow from Wittenham Clumps (Walk 26)
East Hendred (Walk 29)

traffic lights onto a road to: "Headington Hospitals: TAVR Centre". At a T-junction bear right along The Slade. In ¹/₃ mile turn right down Wood Farm Road; 150 yards later, swing right into Atkyns Road.

Terrain: Gradual ascents and descents. Walk A: three stiles. Walk B: no stiles.

Refreshments: Wheatley: The Sun (Pubmaster) 01865-872264 G, CA in G.

Public Transport: Oxford City Centre - Wood Farm 7B(T), 15(O/CL) daily.

Walk A (6¹/₂ miles)

Route:

1.   With your back to the shops, turn left and walk to the end of Atkyns Road. Follow a tarmac path into a wood. When the path divides, take the left fork and soon reach a road with houses on the far side (Broad Oak). Turn left. At the end, swing right along a path across Broad Oak Nature Park leading to the Eastern Bypass. Carefully cross the bypass and enter SHOTOVER COUNTRY PARK.

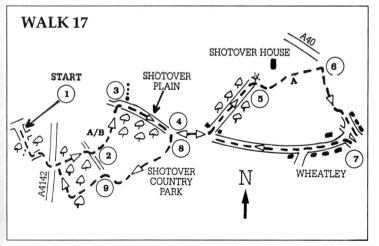

WALK 17

Go straight ahead on a wide, ascending, tarmac track. Ignore all side paths. After $^1/_4$ mile come to a T-junction with a similar track. Bear right and in 100 yards pass through a large wooden gate into an unmade road (The Ridings). Turn right.

2.   Fifty yards along the road our route branches left onto a bridleway (marked by blue arrows) climbing between trees and a garden. When the path reaches woodland, look back for wide ranging views over Oxford to Boars Hill, Didcot power station, the Downs and Chilterns. Continue uphill to arrive at a junction of eight paths. Maintain course, taking one of a pair of ascending, parallel paths running close together. Ignore all side tracks. At the summit, where the path turns right by some large trees, walk forwards through the woodland to a car park. This is Shotover Plain - a broad, grassy ride traversing the summit of Shotover Hill and once the road from Oxford to London and favourite haunt of highwaymen.

3.   The route bears right here and follows an unmade road along the plain. After about $^1/_4$ mile, walk over to a gap in the line of trees on your left and enjoy fine views to the north. Beckley TV mast is on the left. In $^1/_2$ mile come to the end of the plain.

4.   Continue along the unmade road, now running between hedges. One hundred yards beyond a reservoir which looks like a flat-topped grassy mound, turn left through imposing double wooden gates beside lodge houses. A splendid tree-lined avenue descends from here for $^1/_2$ mile to SHOTOVER HOUSE. On the way glorious views open up on your right across the Thame valley to the Chilterns. This was the original approach to Shotover House from the Old London Road.

5.   At the end of the avenue, go forwards through an iron gate to William Kent's ornamental temple set on a grassy knoll. After viewing the temple and catching a glimpse of the house and formal gardens, return through the iron gate (N.B. Only the temple is open to the public; the gardens are private.) Turn left. The track descends to a tarmac drive. Walk ahead, following the drive to the far end of farm buildings. Do not turn left here but take a farm track going half left between fields. In 200 yards come to a junction with a metalled drive. Turn right. Look left from the drive to see the other side of Shotover House, a long narrow lake and an ornamental Gothic

temple.

6.   At the end of the drive turn right onto a signposted footpath ("Wheatley ³/₄"). Climb a stile and aim half right over a field. Halfway across, another stile becomes visible in a wire fence on the opposite side. Beyond this, the path goes ahead over the next field towards a large house. On the far side enter the village of Wheatley. Proceed along a road for 100 yards until it divides. Take the left fork (Westfield Road) and in 50 yards arrive at the Sun pub. Veer left here along Church Road. After 100 yards reach the unique lock-up - a hexagonal pyramid crowned with a ball. It was built by a local mason in 1834. The playground behind, once a quarry, served as a bull-baiting and cock-fighting pit during the 19th century.

Wheatley: the lock-up

7.   From here you can explore the remainder of the village before returning to the Sun via Church Road. Continue down the left-hand side of the inn past the ends of Kiln Lane and High Street to enter Littleworth Road. Follow this road for ¹/₃ mile, passing a school on your right. At a point where the main road veers sharply left, keep straight on along Old Road (signposted "Shotover only").

Climb up the old stagecoach route for 1 mile to reach Shotover Plain, the final $1/4$ mile retracing our outward journey. Immediately swing left at a wooden notice: "Shotover Country Park".

8.   The path re-enters woodland between two metal posts on the right and a red fire warning on the left. Once inside the woods, turn left and follow a bridleway leading downhill. The route is marked with blue arrows. Ignore all side tracks. Eventually exit the wood via a bridge over a stream. Follow the track around two sides of a field, turning right at the corner. Pass across a second field and enter a narrow tarmac road on the edge of woodland.

9.   Turn left along the road. After 100 yards note a green and white marker on the right-hand side. Bear left here onto a bridleway through the wood. In $1/3$ mile swing right onto a farm track running along the edge of the wood. Continue for $1/4$ mile to a T-junction with a tarmac path. Turn left, cross over the Eastern Bypass and retrace your steps to the start.

Walk B (3 miles)

Route:

Follow Instructions 1 to 3 of Walk A, to reach point 4 on the map. At the end of the plain, turn right at a wooden notice: "Shotover Country Park". Now follow Instructions 8 and 9 of Walk A.

Points of Interest

SHOTOVER COUNTRY PARK A 400 acre site on the south-facing slope of Shotover Hill managed by Oxford City Council for public enjoyment. Once part of the medieval royal forest of Shotover, this beautiful area of woodland, heath, meadow and marsh supports an amazing diversity of wildlife, including some rare species. Accordingly, it has been designated as a Site of Special Scientific Interest. Badger, fox, grey squirrel and muntjac deer have all made their home here. Birds spotted in the park include: yellowhammer, green woodpecker, goldfinch, goldcrest, firecrest, kestrel, sparrowhawk, fieldfare and redwing. Part of the land surface consists of an acidic, sandy soil where heather flourishes. Other flora include: bluebell, wood anemone, violet, primrose, lesser celandine, yellow archangel, heath bedstraw, St John's wort and spotted orchid. Three waymarked nature trails visit the important wildlife habitats.

SHOTOVER HOUSE The house, built by Sir James Tyrell between 1714 and 1718, is set in formal gardens of considerable interest, originally laid out with extensive avenues and cross walks. A narrow lake created a vista from the house to a small temple - one of the earliest Gothic garden features. From 1734 William Kent reshaped the western half of the park, building an octagonal temple on a grassy knoll at the highest point of the garden, an obelisk, and an octagonal pond. All were joined by long avenues. Today the layout is largely as it was in the 1730s - a rare example of the last phase of formal landscape design. The gardens are open once a year in aid of the National Gardens Scheme.

WALK 18

Cumnor - Farmoor Reservoir

(5 miles)

Heading westwards from the thatched cottages of Cumnor this attractive walk soon opens up some splendid views across the wide expanse of Farmoor Reservoir - home to a rich variety of water birds. More birdlife is encountered as you continue along a quiet stretch of the Thames to the ancient ferry crossing at Bablock Hythe before returning to the start.

O.S. Maps:	Landranger 164. Pathfinder 1116.
Start (461,042):	Park and start at the post office, High Street, Cumnor (near to the church). 3¹/₂ miles W of Oxford on the A420.
Terrain:	Level and easy gradients. Twelve stiles.
Refreshments:	Cumnor: Bear and Ragged Staff (Free House) 01865-862329 SDA, G, CA, DA in G. S.
Public Transport:	Oxford-Abingdon 4B(O/CL) M-Sat. Oxford-Swindon 42, 66(TD, SD, TA) M-Sat.

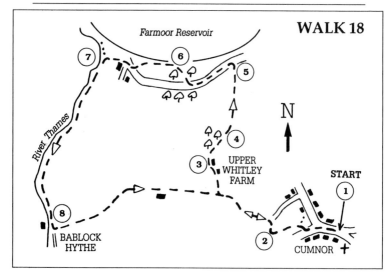

WALK 18

Farmoor Reservoir

River Thames

UPPER
WHITLEY
FARM

BABLOCK
HYTHE

START

CUMNOR

Route:

1.   With your back to the post office turn left and walk down
CUMNOR High Street. Just past the war memorial, branch left into
Appleton Road. After 60 yards cross the road and, keeping a pond
on your left, take a narrow, signposted path between garden walls.
In 20 yards turn left over a stile into a long, narrow field. Our route
follows the left-hand edge of this field, crosses a stile at the far end
and then keeps to the right-hand edge of the next field. When the
field boundary starts to curve left, turn sharply right. Pass between
a hedge and a small stone building to enter a driveway.

2.   Proceed along the driveway to reach a tarmac lane. Swing left
here onto a bridleway signposted to Bablock Hythe. The track
gradually descends, allowing glimpses of Farmoor Reservoir
through gaps in the hedge on your right. After $1/4$ mile take a right-
hand fork to Upper Whitley Farm and follow a drive up to the
farmhouse.

3.   Opposite the house, go through a waymarked gate at the far
end of a tennis court. Bear right across a small paddock to a stile.
Beyond the stile, cross a concrete road and walk forwards on a

Cumnor: the bridleway to Bablock Hythe

broad, grassy track for 40 yards to the end of the last farm building. Turn right. In 50 yards pass through a waymarked gate and walk downhill, keeping close to the wood on your left.

4.   After 150 yards, the wood gives way to a fence. Climb a stile in the fence to enter a field on your left. Our route continues on a downward gradient across the field to a gap in the hedge opposite. Cross a stile and footbridge. Keep going in the same direction over the next field, aiming for the right-hand end of a hedge. Pass under power cables and enjoy a good view of woods on Wytham Hill, ahead. At the hedge (footpath sign here) veer slightly left onto a track following the left-hand field boundary. Farmoor Reservoir soon comes into view. Leave the field via a stile and enter a road.

5.   A small diversion can be made over the stile opposite to a picnic area with tables and chairs, overlooking the reservoir. Otherwise, turn left along the road. After $1/4$ mile swing right through a gate onto a waymarked path through Bushy Leaze Copse. On the far side, the track goes over a footbridge before climbing along the right-hand edge of a field.

6. At the top of the incline the reservoir comes back into view. Follow the path through young trees and over a stile at the field end. Turn right along a road for 30 yards. Climb another stile immediately to the right of a detached house and pass alongside the house. Fifty yards farther on the route crosses a footbridge and stile to enter a long, narrow field. Proceed forwards and soon arrive at the Thames.

7. Turn left along the towpath. Mobile homes on the far bank are a visual intrusion but there is still much to enjoy while strolling through the lush water-meadows beside a lazily meandering river. After 1 mile climb a stile into a bridleway. This is Bablock Hythe - a crossing point of the river since Roman times and favourite haunt of Matthew Arnold; he refers to "crossing the stripling Thames at Bablockhithe" in his pastoral elegy *The Scholar-Gipsy*. Nowadays there is no regular ferry service but the Ferryman Inn, on the opposite bank, does have a boat which can carry passengers.

8. Turn left along the bridleway, signposted: "Cumnor 2". Tall hedges enclose the ancient trail as it gently winds its way uphill away from the river. After $^1/_2$ mile, the hedges give way to an open field. Soon pass Long Leys Farm and rejoin the outward path back to Cumnor.

Points of Interest

CUMNOR The name is said to mean "Cuma's hillside" after an 8th century abbot of Abingdon Abbey. In the 14th or 15th century the abbey built Cumnor Place next to the church as a summer retreat for its abbots. After the Dissolution, Anthony Forster, steward of Robert Dudley (later Earl of Leicester), occupied the house for a time. A favourite of Queen Elizabeth, Dudley spent most of his time at court, his wife, Amy Robsart, being sadly neglected. In 1560, while staying with Forster and his household at Cumnor Place, Amy was discovered dead at the foot of a staircase. The cause of her death remains a mystery. Was it an accident or was she murdered to allow Dudley to seek the Queen's hand? Whatever the truth of the matter, Sir Walter Scott made use of the story in his novel *Kenilworth*. Cumnor Place was eventually demolished in 1811. All that remains today is a stone fireplace, decorated with tiny quatrefoils, set in a bank of the churchyard extension.

St Michael's church contains two items associated with the life and times of Amy Robsart: a life-size statue of Queen Elizabeth and a monument to Anthony Forster. Other objects worthy of perusal include a spiral oak staircase (1685), a chained bible and 15th century stalls with superbly carved poppy-heads.

FARMOOR RESERVOIR A pair of artificial lakes covering 364 acres, filled from the Thames. At weekends the reservoir becomes a colourful spectacle as sailing boats and sailboards take to the water. At the same time fishermen line its banks to seek out trout from the depths. Over 200 species of birds have been recorded at Farmoor. Cormorant, goosander and golden-eye winter here, while arctic, black and common terns and various waders are seen in springtime, with martins, swifts and swallows appearing during the summer. To see more of the reservoir, diversions can be made by turning right at the picnic area or towpath.

WALK 19
Sunningwell - Boars Hill
(5¹/₂ miles)

Starting in the quiet, attractive village of Sunningwell this walk climbs up Boars Hill and explores the superb views visible from Matthew Arnold's beloved "Cumner hills" - including the "dreaming spires of Oxford", "the Vale" (of White Horse) and "Ilsley Downs" (North Wessex Downs). The route progresses via field paths, leafy lanes and woodland tracks to the final vantage point of Jarn Mound before returning to the start.

O.S. Maps:	Landranger 164. Pathfinder 1116.
Start (495,005):	St Leonard's church, Sunningwell. Park by the church or in the village hall car park opposite. 4 miles SW of Oxford off a minor road to Boars Hill.
Terrain:	Gentle inclines; two easy hill climbs. One stile.
Refreshments:	Boars Hill: The Fox (Greenalls) 01865-735131

SDA, G, PA, CA, CM, DA in G.

Public Transport: Oxford-Abingdon 104(O/CL) M-F. From Abingdon 114(H) M-F, except Public Hols. Oxford-Abingdon 4B(O/CL) M-Sat to The Bystander (Lower Wootton) then follow a lane for 1 mile to Old Boars Hill (point 8 on the map).

Route:

1.   Before leaving SUNNINGWELL it is well worthwhile exploring this delightful village. You should then return to the church gate, cross the road, and go to the far side of the village hall car park. Enter the field ahead and climb the path straight up BOARS HILL. Pause for a moment at the top and enjoy the panoramic view over Abingdon to the North Wessex Downs before passing through a gate into a tree lined road between large houses.

2.   Follow the road as it continues uphill, firstly turning right (after $^1/_3$ mile) and then left to reach a T-junction with a main road. Turn right. After $^1/_4$ mile bear left at the next junction into Berkeley Road.

3.   In 30 yards swing right through a gate into a field. Cross the field somewhat to the right of the direction indicated by the footpath sign - aiming for an isolated tree on top of a hillock surrounded by an iron fence. Linger here for a while, making use of Gilbert and Mary Murray's seat, and enjoy one of the finest views over the "dreaming spires of Oxford". Our route continues towards Oxford and the far right-hand corner of the field. Climb a stile here hidden beneath trees and turn left.

4.   Follow a path along the left-hand edge of a field. Go through a metal gate at the far end and across the corner of the next field. Pass through a second metal gate. Continue for $^1/_2$ mile along the right-hand edge of three further fields before passing through a small metal gate into a farm track near to Chilswell Farm. Turn left towards the farm. Inside the farm buildings bear left and soon pass a red brick/wooden house on your right. Continue along the farm track as it turns right and proceeds gently uphill. Open fields on the left stretch away to the wooded summit of Boars Hill while splendid views of Oxford are to be had through gaps in the hedge on your right.

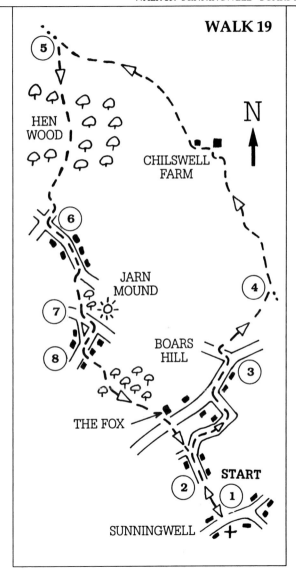

WALK 19

N

5

HEN
WOOD

CHILSWELL
FARM

6

JARN
MOUND

7

4

8

BOARS
HILL

3

THE FOX

2

START

1

SUNNINGWELL

5.   After $^3/_4$ mile turn sharply left off the main track onto a bridleway across an open field. Pass under electricity power lines and enter Hen Wood. Our route climbs through the wood alongside Youlbury Scout Camp and eventually becomes a metalled lane. A Carmelite priory, telecommunication masts and a reservoir are passed before reaching crossroads.

6.   Turn left on the road signposted to Oxford. After $^1/_4$ mile bear right opposite Masefield House down a narrow path between tall hedges - signposted "Ramblers Jubilee Circular Walk Footpath". Follow the path when it swings left and continues along the left-hand edge of "Matthew Arnold's Field", giving superb views over the Vale of White Horse.

7.   At the end of the field, enter a metalled road and turn left. In 60 yards reach Jarn Garden and Jarn Mound. It is well worth climbing the artificial mound for a final panoramic view of the surrounding countryside. On leaving the garden go straight ahead down a road marked "Old Boars Hill" and gradually descend between houses. After 250 yards Badcock House is reached on your right. Turn left here along a lane past picturesque Yew Cottage with its thatched roof.

8.   The lane soon becomes a narrow footpath gently descending beneath a canopy of trees. When the trees give way to open fields, more fine views appear, with the Downs ahead and Didcot power station prominent on your left. Turn left at the field edge and follow the path adjacent to the woods. In $^1/_4$ mile reach a main road and turn left. After 50 yards, in front of The Fox, cross the road and enter a narrow fenced path between gardens. When the path forks take the right-hand path and soon enter the lane to Sunningwell (point 2 on the map). Retrace your steps back to the starting point.

Points of Interest

SUNNINGWELL Although the church is kept locked, it is well worth entering the churchyard to see the unique seven-sided porch. John Jewel, rector of Sunningwell (1551) and later Bishop of Salisbury, built this most elaborate structure, with its grand Ionic columns, to provide shelter for baptismal parties. In earlier times, Roger Bacon, the famous 13th century scientist and philosopher from Oxford, used the church tower for experiments with his telescopes.

From the church a short walk past the village pond brings you to a large, roomy, black and white building, which until 1950 was the rectory. It is now the Flowing Well Inn. Both inn and village derive their names from a well, which supplies water to the pond. The "Sunning" part of the village name comes from the Anglo-Saxon "Sunningas" tribe - early settlers in the area.

Beyond the pub is a half-timbered manor house, originally built by Benedictine monks in the 16th century. Elizabeth I often resided here when visiting her treasurer, who lived nearby.

BOARS HILL Boars Hill offers a magnificent vantage point from which to view the city of Oxford and surrounding areas. The 50ft-high Jarn Mound, built near the summit by archaeologist Sir Arthur Evans in the 1930s with the aid of unemployed Welsh miners, provides an elevated viewing platform. On a clear day it is claimed that the White Horse Hill, Red Horse Hill in Warwickshire, Wychwood Forest and the Chilterns can be seen from here, but growth of the trees now makes some parts of the panorama less visible than in the past.

Around the mound, Sir Arthur created a wild garden containing native species from all parts of the British Isles. He also gave a large part of his 100-acre Youlbury estate to be a scout camp (passed during the walk). An inscription on a memorial stone at the entrance to the wild garden is a fitting reminder of a distinguished archaeologist and philanthropist: "To Arthur Evans 1851-1941, who loved Antiquity, Nature, Freedom and Youth and made this Viewpoint and Wild Garden for all to enjoy".

Matthew Arnold had popularised the area at the end of the 19th century with his pastoral poems *The Scholar-Gipsy* and *Thyrsis* - both of which drew inspiration from the heathlands of Boars Hill. Early in the 20th century, poets and academics including Arthur Evans, Edmund Blunden, Robert Graves, Gilbert Murray and Poets Laureate John Masefield and Robert Bridges, made their homes here. Others followed and the landscape which inspired Arnold started to disappear. The Oxford Preservation Trust, set up to counter the threat, bought most of the sensitive areas, including "Matthew Arnold's Field", so that today we can still enjoy many of the views which inspired the Victorian poet.

WALK 20

Garsington - Cuddesdon
(Walk A 3^{1}/$_{2}$ miles, Walk B 2^{1}/$_{4}$ miles)

From the picturesque hilltop village of Garsington, the route follows field paths down to the hamlet of Denton - with its thatched cottages and imposing Denton House - before climbing to the peaceful village of Cuddesdon, home of Ripon College. Glorious views over Oxford, rural Oxfordshire and the Chilterns make this a most enjoyable walk.

O.S. Maps:	Landranger 164. Pathfinder 1116.
Start (591,023):	The village cross, The Green, Garsington. Park on The Green. 5 miles SE of Oxford on a minor road.
Terrain:	Gentle inclines. Walk A, fourteen stiles; Walk B, nine stiles.
Refreshments:	Garsington: The Red Lion (Free House), 01865-361413, SDA, G, PA, CA, DA in G, no food Sun evening. Cuddesdon: The Bat and Ball (Free House), 01865-874379, SDA, G, CA.
Public Transport:	Oxford-Watlington 101(T) M-Sat, except Public Hols.

Walk A (3^{1}/$_{2}$ miles)

Route:

1.   From GARSINGTON village cross, walk down the full length of The Green, passing the Old School House on your right. Carry straight on into Southend. After 150 yards turn right into the churchyard. Go to the vantage point at the rear of the church and enjoy extensive views of Oxford, Boars Hill and the Chilterns. The interior of the church is well worth exploring - if open. Return to the road and continue along the elevated roadside path, noting the pond (Gizzle) beneath trees on the opposite side of the road, just

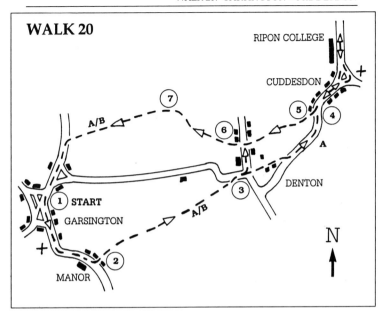

before reaching the splendid Elizabethan manor house. In earlier times the Gizzle was a source of water for many villagers. At Greystone House, a short distance beyond the manor, turn left along a path between houses, signposted "Denton 1".

2.   Behind the houses, the well-trodden path goes straight across a field to a gap in the far hedge. (If freshly ploughed, aim halfway between two sets of trees on the horizon.) After a gentle upward slope the route starts its gradual descent to the hamlet of Denton, crossing two more fields on the way. Note the stone-built mansion of College Farm across fields on your left and Cuddesdon village on the skyline ahead. On entering the final field, aim for the stone wall surrounding Denton House, visible in the far left-hand corner. Our path exits the field at the left-hand end of the wall via a wide gap in the fence and enters a road. Turn right along the road and after 100 yards reach a T-junction. Denton, with its large mansion (Denton House) and picturesque thatched cottages, is on your left.

3.   Go straight ahead over a stile and onto a signposted path across a field. Cross a stile on the far side and go over a stream into a driveway between houses. Continue straight ahead and uphill over an open grassed area to join a quiet country road. Swing left along the road and in ¹/₄ mile enter the hilltop village of CUDDESDON.

4.   After passing the Bat and Ball Inn take the right-hand fork and soon reach the church. The building is well worth exploring. Fine views over the surrounding countryside are to be had from the churchyard. Turn right after leaving the church. In 100 yards join the main road and continue straight ahead. The impressive buildings of Ripon College are on your left, with the most recent addition, Runcie Building (named after a previous Archbishop of Canterbury), being at the far end of the village. A Toc H conference centre (the old Bishops Palace) is on the right. After viewing these, retrace your steps to the road junction. Take the right-hand fork and walk back through the village.

5.   At the far end, 100 yards past a speed limit sign, turn right onto a signposted footpath. Go past a cottage and after 25 yards climb a stile into a field. Our path follows the right-hand edge of the field to a stile at the far end. Go downhill across the next field, aiming for a point 100 yards left of the far right-hand corner. Ahead is the dovecote of Denton House - with its "lighthouse" top. Cross the stile and enter a road. Turn right. After 20 yards bear left at a footpath sign.

6.   In 50 yards climb a stile, cross a narrow field and pass over a second stile. At this point don't fail to notice the unusual sight of Gothic windows - from Brasenose College chapel, Oxford - incorporated into the garden wall of Denton House. Turn three-quarters right and walk across the next field to a stile visible on the far side. Go half left over the following field, aiming first for a wooden electricity pole and then for the far left-hand corner of the field. Look back from mid-field for a good view of Ripon College.

7.   Cross two stiles and a bridge over a stream. Aim for the far right-hand corner of the next field. Climb a stile and follow the right-hand edge of the field ahead. Towards the end of this field climb a stile in the fence on your right and continue uphill along the left-hand edge of the adjacent field. Cross a stile and go over a

narrow field. Climb the final stile and continue uphill for 100 yards to reach a road. Turn left and take the roadside path back to The Green.

Walk B (2¼ miles)

Route:

Follow Instructions 1 and 2 of Walk A, to reach point 3 on the map. At the T-junction turn left and walk along the road through Denton, passing Denton House on your left. About 100 yards further on, turn left onto a signposted footpath. Now follow Walk A from Instruction 6.

Points of Interest

GARSINGTON In spite of modern additions, Garsington retains many fine buildings of historic interest. Foremost amongst these is the church of St Mary, with its original Norman tower, set in a commanding position on the south-west side of the village. A nave and chancel were added in the 13th century. A tombstone in the chancel floor, originally inscribed in Norman French, dates from the same period and commemorates Isabella de la Mare, Lady of the Manor of Garsington. A more recent Lady of the Manor, the beautiful Lady Ottoline Morrell (d. 1938), is also commemorated in a bas-relief to the left of the church door. Outside, note the single-handed tower clock - made by John Thwaites in 1796 and recently restored.

With its enormous yew hedges, immense chimneys and narrow windows, the Elizabethan manor house is considered to be one of the finest of its size in Oxfordshire. Magnificent gardens, situated at the rear, are open to the public twice a year in aid of the National Gardens Scheme. The house came into prominence in the 1920s when Philip Morrell MP and his wife Ottoline were in residence. Lady Ottoline entertained here all the famous literary and artistic figures of the time. Frequent visitors included D.H. Lawrence and his wife Frieda, Aldous Huxley, Siegfried Sassoon, T.S. Eliot, Virginia Woolf, Robert Graves, Bertrand Russell and many more.

CUDDESDON Cuddesdon is a quiet, peaceful village with many stone-built and thatched cottages. Bishops of Oxford lived here at the Old Palace for 400 years, although in recent times the building has become a Toc H conference centre - the bishop preferring to live in Oxford. Presumably one of the reasons for establishing Ripon College here in 1854, as a theological college for training Anglican clergy, was its closeness to the palace. The college buildings, which dominate the northern end of the village, are an uneasy alliance of Victorian and modern architecture.

All Saints parish church is known and loved around the world by thousands of priests as the place where they worshipped God during their time at Ripon College. The interior is kept in beautiful condition. One of the finest features, a Norman arch in the entrance porch, is splendidly carved with zigzags and diamonds.

The Bat and Ball Inn also has an international reputation - in this case for its extensive collection of cricket memorabilia and as a meeting place for cricketers from all parts of the world.

WALK 21

Appleton - River Thames
(Walk A 5¹/₂ miles, Walk B 2 miles)

Appleton, a quiet rural backwater with a Norman manor and charming church, is the starting point for this walk. The route explores beautiful woodland south of the village before heading north for a stroll through verdant meadows beside a tranquil Thames.

O.S. Maps:	Landranger 164. Pathfinder 1116.
Start (443,016):	Park and start at a lay-by in Eaton Road, Appleton, opposite Church Road. 5¹/₂ miles SW of Oxford on a minor road off the A420.
Terrain:	Level and gentle inclines. Walk A: eleven stiles. Walk B: eighteen stiles.
Refreshments:	Appleton: The Thatched Tavern (Brakspear) 01865-864814 SDA, CA, no food M and Sat evenings. The Plough (Morland) 01865-862441 SDA, G, PA, CA, DA in G, no food Tu. S.
Public Transport:	Oxford-Swindon 42, 66(SD, TA, TD) M-Sat.

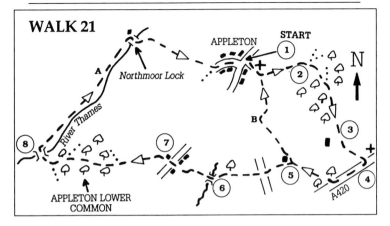

WALK 21

Walk A (5½ miles)

Route:

1.   Walk to the far end of Church Road and follow a path around the church (open). In the churchyard, look over a wall on your right to see the Manor - the oldest house in APPLETON. Our path exits from the rear of the churchyard via a gate, footbridge and stile. Proceed ahead over a narrow field to cross another footbridge and stile. The track continues forwards alongside a fence, at first through an area of scrub and then between fields, to reach woodland.

2.   Ten yards into the wood, branch right off the main track onto a smaller, ascending path winding its way through the trees. In springtime, wood anemone and bluebells add an extra splash of colour to the woodland floor. On approaching the edge of the wood, continue ahead when a second path joins your track from the left. The village of Bessels Leigh can soon be seen across fields on the left-hand side. In 200 yards leave the woodland via a stile.

3.   Walk forwards over a field to a second stile. Beyond this stile turn half left and proceed gently uphill. At the top of the incline aim towards two white gateposts in the distance, next to the busy A420. Bessels Leigh School is hidden behind trees on your right while the village church (locked) and an isolated, stone gatepier can be seen in the left-hand field corner. The gatepier is all that remains of

Bessels Leigh Manor, which once stood where the school stands today. In the 17th century the Manor was owned by William Lenthall, Speaker of the Long Parliament, who defied Charles I when he attempted to arrest five Members of Parliament in 1642 - an event which helped precipitate the Civil War.

4.   Cross a stile beside the white gateposts. Enter the school drive and bear left to reach the A420. Turn right along the roadside verge. In ¹/₄ mile swing right at a footpath sign onto a broad track through woodland. After 50 yards climb a stile and take a narrow path on the left running alongside a fence. At the end of the wood, our route keeps going in the same direction across a field to arrive at Tubney Manor Farm.

5.   Turn left. Follow the field edge around the buildings to a farm drive. Veer left and walk down the drive to reach a metalled road. Cross to the far side. Take a track across the field ahead in the direction of the sign (following the right-hand line of electricity poles). Continue along the left-hand edge of a copse (bluebells here in spring). At the end, turn right through brambles to a bridge over a stream.

6.   Beyond the stream, climb along the right-hand edge of a field. At the corner, bear left for 30 yards before crossing a stile into a paddock. The track goes forwards over the paddock and between gardens to reach a road.

7.   Maintain course across the road and along a bridle-road (Millway). At the last bungalow (Thames View), look over the fence for a fine panorama of the Thames valley. The road gradually winds its way downhill to arrive at the woodland of Appleton Lower Common. Do not veer right here but go straight ahead on a bridleway through the woods. After ¹/₂ mile swing left to join a track coming in from the right. Two hundred yards further on our route leaves the woods and turns right onto a path around a field. Pass under power lines. In 100 yards branch right through a wide gap in a hedge and soon enter a wooded area. Follow the track as it crosses Hart's Weir Footbridge over the Thames.

8.   Turn right along the towpath. Enjoy a pleasant stroll for 1 mile along a peaceful stretch of the river, with only swans and mallards to keep you company. At NORTHMOOR LOCK cross over the lock

116

gates and weir bridge and follow the tarmac access road (not a public right of way but in daily use by villagers) for $^2/_3$ mile back to Appleton. On reaching the village turn left at a T-junction to regain the starting point.

Walk B (2 miles)

Route:

Follow Instructions 1 to 4 of Walk A, to reach point 5 on the map. At Tubney Manor Farm, turn right. Follow a fence around the farm buildings and continue for 100 yards along the left-hand field edge to reach a stile beside a gate. Cross the stile. Our route now goes forwards on a farm track; after 20 yards it turns a quarter left onto a footpath leading towards a stile in the distant hedge, 50 yards left of a gate. The path continues along the left-hand side of the next field. At the corner, turn right and in 100 yards bear left across two stiles and a footbridge. Walk ahead over a paddock. Cross a stile on the far side and go forwards for 30 yards to a second one. Beyond this, take a path following a left-hand field boundary. In 200 yards swing left into the churchyard and return to the start.

Points of Interest

APPLETON A quiet village set on a ridge about one mile south of the Thames. Sixteenth-century thatched cottages agreeably co-exist with more recent dwellings around a central duck pond. Two buildings date from Norman times. One is a rare example of a moated manor house (1190) with a fine Norman doorway. Later additions include a Tudor porch surmounted by a wood-framed upper floor (visible from the churchyard). Few houses in England have a longer record of continuous habitation, the earliest known owner being Mabel de Appleton in 1212. A fine, four-bay, Late Norman arcade (1200) with pointed arches is the oldest part of St Lawrence's church. On the south side of the chancel stands an impressive canopied tomb of Sir John Fettiplace (1593), one time owner of the Manor.

NORTHMOOR LOCK One of the few places on the Thames where you can still see the paddle construction of earlier weirs. Before the invention of pound locks, water flow would be controlled by raising or lowering square-ended paddles set in a wooden framework. For passage of river traffic, paddles and framework could be removed. Boats would then move with the flow downstream or be winched upstream, both operations proving somewhat hazardous.

WALK 22

Buckland - Longworth

(Walk A 9³/₄ miles, Walk B 6¹/₄ miles, Walk C 6 miles)

A ridge of Corallian limestone follows the Thames westwards from Oxford to the county boundary. Walking on the ridge offers fine views and provides an opportunity to visit the attractive villages of Hinton Waldrist, Buckland and Longworth. By way of contrast, ambling through one of the most remote stretches of the Thames valley promotes a feeling of peace and tranquillity. Both types of terrain are included in each walk.

O.S. Maps:	Landranger 164. Pathfinder 1135, 1115.
Start (378,988):	Park and start at the village hall in Hinton Waldrist High Street (beside a bus shelter). 6 miles E of Faringdon on a minor road off the A420.
Terrain:	Level and easy inclines. Walk A: eight stiles. Walk B: two stiles. Walk C: six stiles.
Refreshments:	Buckland: S. Longworth: The Blue Boar (Morrells) 01865-820494 SDA, G, CA, DA.
Public transport:	Oxford-Swindon 66(SD, TD) M-Sat.

Walk A (9³/₄ miles)

Route:

1.   With your back to the village hall, turn right and walk along the High Street out of Hinton Waldrist. Distant views soon open up to the Downs on your left and across the Thames valley on the right. Three hundred yards beyond the village the road curves left.

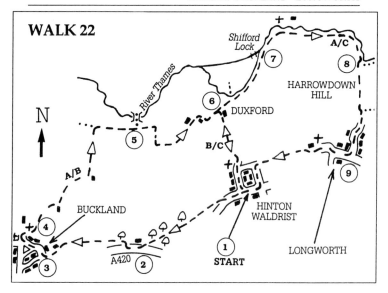

WALK 22

Shifford Lock

HARROWDOWN HILL

DUXFORD

BUCKLAND

HINTON WALDRIST

LONGWORTH

A420

START

N

Continue ahead here onto a gradually descending bridleway. When, after a further 300 yards, the main track veers right, proceed forwards, gently climbing into a pleasant region of woodland and open fields. Ignore all side tracks. After 1 mile join a tarmac drive leading to the A420.

2.   Turn right. Walk along the grass verge for 300 yards past a house and farm drive, before bearing right over a stile onto a signposted footpath ("Buckland 1"). Swing half left across a small field to the top left-hand corner. Climb a wooden fence and join a path leading into the wood on your left. When the trees come to an end, our route maintains course across a wide expanse of open fields to the village of BUCKLAND, visible ahead.

3.   On reaching the village, turn right along a metalled road. In 200 yards come to the centre of Buckland - a pretty collection of thatched, limestone cottages surrounding the Memorial Hall. Follow the main road as it winds its way through the village and arrive at crossroads beside the Roman Catholic church (open). Turn right. Walk 100 yards to a white fence and gate marked "Private". Across

parkland on your left is Buckland House - a splendid building of mellow limestone; in front are the Manor House, with battlemented towers, and the Anglican church (open). Turn right past the church entrance. At the end of two cottages, go through an opening in the wall on your right and follow a left-hand field boundary to a lane. Turn left. Walk downhill out of Buckland, at the same time enjoying a superb panorama of the Thames valley. Wytham Hill is on the right horizon.

4.   Soon pass a sewage works and, $^1/_4$ mile further on, come to a group of farm buildings. Turn left here over an open field; a line of trees marks the route. Part way across, look back for a fine view of Buckland. At the far side, cross a concrete bridge to reach a T-junction. Turn right. Willow trees across the field on your left indicate the line of the River Thames. Our route continues to the field end where a signpost ("Tadpole Bridge $1^1/_2$") points left.

5.   Here you can make a 150 yard diversion to a tranquil spot where Tenfoot Bridge spans the river; otherwise proceed ahead. In 250 yards bear right at a bridleway sign over a small stone bridge and alongside an overgrown hedge. After 100 yards the track veers first left and then right through a break in the hedge to maintain course along the right side of the adjacent field. One hundred yards further on, turn left across the field. On the far side pass through a gap in a line of trees and keep going in the same direction along the right-hand side of the next field. When the field comes to an end walk through another line of trees. The track leads forwards past Duxford Farm, soon becoming a metalled lane. Follow this winding lane for $^1/_3$ mile to reach an unusually tall, thatched cottage.

6.   Turn left here onto a signposted bridleway. In 200 yards come to Duxford Ford - a delightfully secluded spot where weeping willows cascade down into the water and you may be tempted to linger awhile. Turn right. A flight of steps quickly takes us up to a higher level. Our track then follows the river bank for $^2/_3$ mile to arrive at a wooden footbridge leading to Shifford Lock and Weir.

7.   Do not cross, but maintain course ahead. For the next $1^1/_2$ miles we keep alongside a river meandering over a flat, open country, whose flatness is disturbed only by clumps of pollarded willow. In $^1/_3$ mile you are opposite Shifford church - standing all alone in the

fields. Its related hamlet is some distance away to the right. According to early records, Alfred once convened the English Parliament here: "there sat at Shifford many thanes, many bishops, and many learned men, wise earls, and awful knights". Beyond Shifford the path crosses four fields. At the far side of the fourth field, go through a gate at the left-hand end of a row of pollarded willows. The path continues alongside the river towards Harrowdown Hill. On reaching a pair of gates enclosing a footbridge (the river swings sharply left here), turn right along the field edge. In 100 yards, cross a stile and start the ascent of Harrowdown Hill.

8.　At first, the path follows a right-hand field boundary. Look back from the top of the field for a Thames valley panorama. Continue between hedges to the highest point (295ft, 90m) and enjoy views of Wytham Hill, Cumnor Hurst and Boars Hill to the east with the top of Didcot power station peeping over the southern horizon. A broad track leads down from the summit towards Longworth - visible on the skyline. At the first house on your right, bear left for 30 yards before swinging right and climbing into the village. Pass Glebe Cottage and the Blue Boar Inn to reach a T-junction. Turn right.

9.　After 200 yards the main road curves left. Swing right here onto a lane signposted: "Longworth Church and bridlepath to Hinton Waldrist". In $^1/_4$ mile arrive at the church. Bear half left through the wrought iron gates of 17th century Longworth Manor and walk past the house, well kept gardens and farm buildings. Veer right around the last building. Twenty yards further on, the bridleway swings left towards Hinton Waldrist and becomes a ridgeway with fine views on either side. At the village, turn left along Priors Lane and in 400 yards come to a crossroads. Bear right here to reach the starting point.

Walk B (6$^1/_4$ miles)

Route:
Follow Instructions 1 to 5 of Walk A to reach point 6 on the map. Continue along the lane as it curves right past the thatched cottage and gradually ascends to Hinton Waldrist, $^3/_4$ mile distant. At the church, keep going in the same direction to arrive at the High Street and our starting point.

Walk C (6 miles)
Route:
With your back to the village hall turn right and walk along the High Street. In 100 yards turn right again. Maintain course past the church and soon enjoy an expansive view to the right, with Harrowdown Hill (climbed later) in the foreground. Three-quarters of a mile further on arrive at an unusually tall, thatched cottage. Bear right here onto a signposted bridleway. Now follow Walk A from the second sentence of Instruction 6.

Points of Interest

BUCKLAND Pretty thatched cottages blend with more recent dwellings to form a village of charm and character. On the northwest side of Buckland stands the magnificent, neo-classical edifice of Buckland House - built by John Wood the Younger (creator of the Royal Crescent at Bath) for Sir John Throckmorton in 1757. The wings were added in 1910. Beautiful parkland surrounding the house is open to the public once a year in aid of the National Gardens Scheme. Dating from Norman times, St Mary's church was later extended to include a chancel, transepts and a fine battlemented tower. The church is entered through a splendid arched doorway in the original Norman nave to reveal a lovely interior. In 1890, William West, a wealthy director of the Great Western Railway, transformed the south transept into a spectacular mosaic memorial to his wife Clara Jane. Behind St Mary's lies the 16th century Manor House - given a Gothic face-lift in the 18th century.

WALK 23

Buscot - Kelmscott

(4¹/₂ miles)

A short walk connecting the Thames-side villages of Buscot and Kelmscott - the latter being the 19th century home of William Morris. Both settlements are typical of the Cotswold region. The outward route is by way of field paths while the return leg follows a meandering river through a peaceful countryside.

O.S. Maps:	Landranger 163. Pathfinder 1135.
Start (231,978):	Buscot Weir National Trust car park, Buscot. 4 miles W of Faringdon on the A417.
Terrain:	Level. Ten stiles.
Refreshments:	Buscot: Tearoom/shop, G, Tu-Sat all day, Sun afternoon. Kelmscott: The Plough Inn (Free House) 01367-253543 SDA, Restaurant, G, CA, CM, DA, daily 11-11.
Public Transport:	From Swindon and Faringdon 67(TD) F. Buses also call at Lechlade, 1 mile by footpath from point 3 on the walk.

Route:

1.   From the car park, turn right and follow a narrow road towards BUSCOT weir. On approaching the Thames, branch right towards a bridge. To visit Buscot church (locked) and Old Parsonage, you need to make a 300 yard leftward diversion just before the bridge; otherwise cross to the far side and turn right past Lock Cottage. The

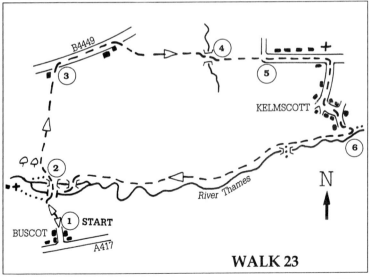

WALK 23

path now leads over a weir, through trees and gardens, across Buscot Lock gates and forwards over a second weir to enter Gloucestershire.

2.   Cross a stile into the field ahead. Bear half left and walk towards the steeple of Lechlade church. After 150 yards turn right through an opening in a double barbed wire fence. Fifty yards away across the field is a large gap in a hedge and row of trees. The obvious route proceeds forwards through the gap and continues along a farm track. However, the official path goes over two stiles and footbridges, 30 yards left of the gap, before joining the farm track. In $1/2$ mile pass Leaze Farm and come to the B4449. Turn right.

3.   Walk along the road for $1/4$ mile to reach farm buildings on your right. After passing the final barn, turn right at a footpath sign and climb a stile into a field. Aim for a wide metal gate in the far left-hand corner. Beyond the gate our route turns half left and follows a hedge along the left-hand field boundary before crossing a stile in the field corner. Continue in the same direction through the next field. When the hedge comes to an end, go forwards across the field for 100 yards to a stream. Turn right. In a few yards, swing left onto a bridge over the stream and re-enter Oxfordshire.

4.   If the path across the next field is not visible, turn a quarter right and aim for the far right-hand corner, slightly to the right of a cottage. (If the route is blocked by crops, turn right, follow the stream to a farm track and then turn left.) Pass through a gap in the distant hedge and bear right onto a road leading into KELMSCOTT.

5.   In $1/3$ mile come to the church, burial place of William Morris. On leaving the church, go left for a few yards before branching right towards The Plough. At the inn veer left for 30 yards to a point where the road divides. Take the left fork past Memorial Cottages - built by Jane Morris in 1902 in memory of her husband and identified by a carved relief of Morris on the front. Turn right at the next fork to arrive at the grey stone Manor House - Morris's old home. Beyond the manor, a broad track continues down to the Thames, some 200 yards distant.

6.   Turn right here onto the towpath. For the next $1^3/4$ miles we can enjoy some pleasant riverside scenery on the way back to Buscot. From the first section of path Buscot House is visible, $1^1/4$ miles away

Kelmscott: carved relief of William Morris on the Memorial Cottages

across the river. Further on, the trees and folly atop Faringdon Hill stand out on the left-hand skyline. In $^{1}/_{2}$ mile come to Eaton Weir Bridge, with its tiny cottage and moored boats of the Anchor Boat Club - a name that reminds us of the Anchor Inn which once stood here. Sadly, it was destroyed by fire many years ago. Do not cross the bridge but continue alongside the river. As you walk, look out for a pair of Buscot Park gatehouses, across fields on the left. Finally swing left over a concrete bridge and follow the path through a small meadow to arrive at Buscot Lock - a delightful spot to rest awhile before returning to the car park.

Points of Interest

BUSCOT A small limestone village, $^{1}/_{4}$ mile south of the Thames, owned by the National Trust. When rebuilt by the first Lord Faringdon in the 1890s, Buscot gained a four-gabled roof over the village well and a solid-looking village hall surmounted by a clock-tower and cupola. The church and Old Parsonage (1703) stand beside the Thames, $^{1}/_{2}$ mile north-west of the village. Of late Norman origin, St Mary's boasts a fine Perpendicular tower and porch. One mile south-east of Buscot lies Buscot House (1780), built in the Adam style. It is set in fine parkland with magnificent water gardens and a great lake (see **Appendix C** for opening times).

KELMSCOTT A remote, unspoilt, straggling village which is literally at the end of the road to "Nowhere", as described by William Morris. Morris fell in love with the place and made his country home here. During his life he was at one time, poet, writer, artist, craftsman, designer, publisher, social reformer and manufacturer. Wallpapers and fabrics to the designs of Morris and Co remain popular today. The handsome, gabled Manor House with mullioned windows, where Morris lived from 1871 to 1896, contains a fascinating collection of his works (see **Appendix C** for opening times).

A simple cruciform church lies at the village centre. Dedicated to St George, whose portrayal in medieval glass (1430) can be seen behind the altar, the north transept is decorated with red ochre paintings from about 1280. On the south-east side of the churchyard, a plain, ridge-shaped tomb marks William Morris's final resting place.

WALK 24

Coleshill - Great Coxwell

(6 miles)

From the National Trust village of Coleshill our route climbs through fields and woods to Badbury Hill - the site of an Iron Age hill-fort and an excellent vantage point. Dropping down to Great Coxwell brings us to one of the finest tithe barns in England. We return through the Vale of White Horse, enjoying some good views of the Downs on the way.

O.S. Maps: Landranger 163. Pathfinder 1135.
Start (236,938):   Park and start at Coleshill church. 4 miles W of
                     Faringdon on the B4019.

Terrain:	Gentle inclines. Twelve stiles.
Refreshments:	Coleshill: The Radnor Arms (The National Trust/Discovery Inns) 01793-762366 SDA, G, CA, DA. S.
Public Transport:	Swindon-Faringdon-Ashbury 67(TD) F.

Route:

1. From COLESHILL church walk back to the main road and turn left. At The Radnor Arms, swing left along a narrow lane. In 150 yards join a minor road. Cross to the far side and bear right onto a signposted footpath which passes through a gap in a line of trees. Gradually climb uphill, following the left-hand edge of the field ahead. As you gain height, extensive views open up over Oxfordshire, Wiltshire and Gloucestershire on your left. Our route continues in the same direction along the edge of a second field, through a copse, and by the side of a third field, to reach a path enclosed by hedges and fences. Beyond a stile at the distant end of this path, swing left and proceed 30 yards to a field corner. Turn right here. After 60 yards cross a stile into an adjacent field. Go half right across the field, aiming for the right-hand edge of farm buildings. At the far side, climb a stile and turn right onto a farm

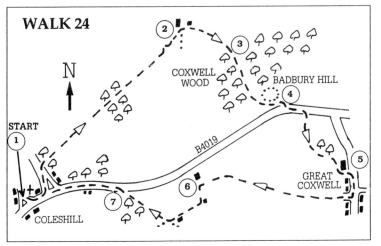

track.

2.   Pass through two metal gates alongside Brimstone Farm to arrive at a concrete farm road. Walk straight across and through a gate into a field. Follow the left field edge past Brimstone Farmhouse. At the distant end, cross a concrete bridge and go through a metal gate. Turn left. Proceed 30 yards to the field corner and swing right. The path now keeps to the field boundary as it ascends towards Coxwell Wood.

3.   Once inside the wood, our path becomes wider and steeper. Continue uphill, crossing two broad tracks. Just before reaching the summit, a clearing affords good views to the right. Ignore all side tracks. The main path gradually levels out and curves right and then left before coming to Badbury Hill National Trust car park. The Iron Age fort is on your left. Masses of bluebells enlighten the woodland scene here in late spring. From the car park and fort there are extensive views to the Downs, Faringdon Hill, Vale of White Horse and the upper Thames valley.

4.   Proceed through the car park to the B4019. Turn left. In 200 yards bear right over a stile onto a path signposted: "Great Coxwell ¹/₂". A wide track leads across an open field towards the right-hand end of a wood. On reaching the wood, continue ahead along the field edge. Just before the field corner, swing left over a stile into the trees. A path crosses the corner of the wood to a stile on the far side. Beyond the stile, turn left and follow the field edge to another stile giving access to GREAT COXWELL BARN.

5.   After viewing the building, leave by the main entrance and turn right into the village. At the centre, our route bears right down Puddleduck Lane. A diversion can be made by continuing forwards to the oldest part of the village around the 12th century church of St Giles (locked). Puddleduck Lane climbs out of the village and soon becomes a bridleway offering glorious views of White Horse Hill and the Downs. For the first mile our route passes between hedges, across an open field and along the right-hand boundary of a second field. At the field end, go through a metal gate into a farm track. Colleymore Farm is on your right.

6.   Turn left. Walk down the hedge-lined track for 200 yards to a red brick house. Bear right here through a metal gate. Proceed along

The Downs above Blewbury (Walk 30)
Bluebells in Oaken Copse (Walk 32)

Bix valley (Walk 34)
Hernes valley (Walk 36)

the right-hand edge of two fields to arrive at Ashen Copse Farm. Pass to the right of the farm buildings. Come to a T-junction with a metalled lane and turn right. In $^1/_3$ mile reach the B4019.

7.   Swing left onto a broad grass verge beside the road. The impressive Coleshill Gates soon appear on your left. A short diversion through the gates reveals some fine views across Coleshill Park. Back on the road, it is but a short distance to the starting point in Coleshill village.

Points of Interest

COLESHILL According to local folklore, the name originates from Old King Cole of nursery rhyme fame who once made merry hereabouts. Clinging to a hillside above the River Cole, this fine stone village looks out over Wiltshire, the best views being obtained from the churchyard. All Saints church, a Norman foundation with a Perpendicular tower, was extensively restored by the Earl of Radnor in 1782. The second Earl, who rebuilt the village about 1870, is remembered together with his forebear in the name of its inn - The Radnor Arms. A picture of Coleshill House, an elegant mansion destroyed by fire in 1952 which once stood above the village, hangs from a wall inside the hostelry. Designed by Inigo Jones with help from Roger Pratt, the house was built betweeen 1650 and 1662; according to Pevsner, it "...was the best Jonesian mid-17th century house in England". Entrance gates to the mansion ("Coleshill Gates") are passed during our walk.

GREAT COXWELL BARN "As noble as a cathedral" is how William Morris described it. This magnificent structure, one of the longest medieval tithe barns in England, is over 150ft (45m) long and more than 50ft (15m) high. Four foot (1.3m) thick limestone walls and an interior frame of oak posts on stone bases, held together by tie beams, roof plates and bracing struts, support a roof of Cotswold stone tiles. Most of the woodwork is original.

In 1204 King John granted the Manor of Faringdon, including Great Coxwell, to Beaulieu Abbey, a Cistercian foundation in Hampshire. Monks from the abbey established a cell here and built the barn about 1250. It was bequeathed to the National Trust in 1956.

Great Coxwell tithe barn: interior structure

WALK 25

Abingdon - Sutton Courtenay
(Walk A 7¹/₄ miles, Walk B 6¹/₄ miles)

Pastoral stretches of the Thames combine with the noble buildings of historic Abingdon and rustic charm of Sutton Courtenay to make this a pleasurable walk at all seasons of the year. Two-thirds of the route is by way of riverside paths.

O.S. Maps:	Landranger 164. Pathfinder 1136.
Start (500,968):	Car park (with toilets) on the south side of Abingdon Bridge.
Terrain:	Mostly level. Walk A: eight stiles. Walk B: six stiles.
Refreshments:	Abingdon: a wide range available. Culham: Waggon and Horses (Whitbread) 01235-525012 SDA, G, PA, CA, CM, DA in G, 11-11. Sutton Courtenay: George and Dragon (Morland) 01235-848252 SDA, G, CA.
Public Transport:	From Oxford: X3, 35/A (O/CL) daily; 31, X31 (T) daily. From Oxford and Henley: 390 (T) daily.

Walk A (7¹/₄ miles)

Route:

1.   From the car park walk towards Abingdon Bridge. Immediately after passing two houses, turn right through a small iron gate set in the bridge wall and drop down to the towpath. Bear right. At first, our route follows the river to Abingdon lock and weir. On approaching the weir, look back for a classic view of the riverside scene. Keep going in the same direction past the lock and through a wooden gate. The path is now in open country. In ¹/₄ mile another, smaller, weir marks the start of one branch of SWIFT DITCH - a quiet stretch of water partly hidden by bulrushes and water lilies.

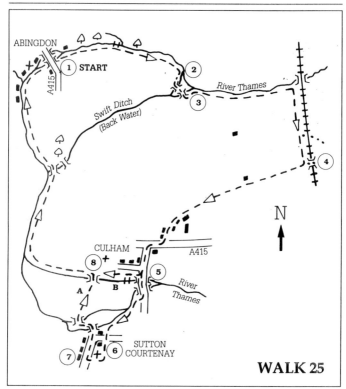

WALK 25

2.   Our track veers right here and after 200 yards it forks. Take the left branch over a wooden bridge crossing Swift Ditch. One hundred yards further on, the route divides again. This time take the right track through a narrow gap between bushes, towards the sound of running water. Here the masonry of one of the first pound locks on the Thames lies beneath a wooden bridge spanning a second branch of Swift Ditch (an information board provides historical details). Cross this bridge and a second one before bearing left along a field edge to regain the river's bank.

3.   Our path now swings right and follows the Thames for ³/₄ mile to a railway embankment carrying Brunel's London to Oxford line.

Turn right here. Climb along the field boundary and cross two stiles. Look back from the second one. The Thames flood plain can be seen stretching away to your left, with St Helen's spire (Abingdon) in the distance, while Boars Hill rises up in front. The path continues beside the railway, soon becoming a farm track. In $^1/_4$ mile ignore a side path to the left. Three hundred yards further on, arrive at a T-junction with Thame Lane. The light coloured buildings of Culham Laboratory (a centre for environmental and nuclear fusion research) are across the bridge on your left. Didcot power station lies over the fields ahead, with the Downs behind.

4.   Turn right. After $^3/_4$ mile pass the European School and soon reach the busy A415. Bear right for 200 yards before turning left at traffic lights. Proceed downhill through the edge of Culham village to arrive at more traffic lights next to a bridge.

5.   Maintain course, crossing road bridges over Culham Cut and the Thames. Fifty yards beyond the second bridge, branch right through a wooden kissing gate into a meadow. Turn half left. Follow a tranquil path beside the Thames for $^1/_4$ mile to reach a stile. On the far side, a concrete lane curves left alongside a wall towards a gate and a second stile.

6.   Cross the stile into SUTTON COURTENAY. Proceed ahead over a road and down All Saints Lane, left of The Fish Inn. In 200 yards come to the back wall of All Saints churchyard. Enter through double iron gates. Famous author George Orwell and Lord Asquith, the last Liberal Prime Minister (1908 to 1916), are buried here. To find their graves, turn left alongside the wall. Twenty yards short of the corner, turn right and walk forwards for about 20 yards to find the simple grave of Eric Arthur Blair (Orwell's real name). Continue on towards the church. The substantial tomb of Herbert Henry Asquith stands 15 yards to the right of a large yew tree. Ten yards nearer the church is the resting place of 117 year-old Martha Pye, who died in 1822. Keep going past the church and out of the churchyard into the Green - a most delectable spot.

7.   Turn right. Walk to the end of Church Street, passing the George and Dragon and a fascinating variety of houses and cottages on the way. When the road turns right, bear half left onto a footpath beside a wall. Soon pass through a gate. Follow this delightful path

The mill stream, Sutton Courtenay

beneath a canopy of trees as it winds its way across weirs, with attractive gardens and a mill stream on the left, and Sutton Pools - part of the Thames - on your right. The track continues for ¼ mile over open fields before crossing a footbridge straddling Culham Cut. Turn left.

8.   Our route keeps to the towpath for the next 1³/₄ miles, first along Culham Cut and then beside the river. After 1 mile cross a wooden footbridge over Swift Ditch next to old Culham Bridge (1416). The spire of St Helen's church in ABINGDON is now visible ahead and houses soon appear on the opposite bank. This approach to the town provides superb views of one of the finest river fronts on the Thames. Features to note include: an iron bridge over the River Ock where it enters the Thames, red brick almshouses surrounding The Old Anchor Inn, St Helen's church, beautiful town houses with gardens stretching down to the river, the hexagonal Old Gaol and Abingdon Bridge (1416, last rebuilt in 1927). Immediately beyond the bridge, turn right up a flight of stone steps to regain the starting point.

Walk B (6¼ miles)

Route:

Follow Instructions 1 to 4 of Walk A to reach point 5 on the map. Turn right through a small gate. The towpath goes past Culham Lock and alongside Culham Cut. In ¼ mile it arrives at a foot-bridge over the cut. Continue ahead here, following Walk A from Instruction 8.

Points of Interest

SWIFT DITCH At one time the Thames above Abingdon split into two navigable channels, one through the town, the other along Swift Ditch. By the early 17th century, both routes had many shallows and were impassable to large boats. When Commissioners, charged with improving navigation below Oxford, had to choose a preferred route, they selected Swift Ditch. Here, about 1630, one of the first three pound locks (the modern type of lock with two gates) was constructed on the Thames. The remains of this lock, now the oldest of its type in the country, are passed during the walk. To bring traffic back through the town, citizens of Abingdon built a lock on their branch of the river in 1790 and Swift Ditch fell into disuse.

SUTTON COURTENAY A beautiful village of charming houses and cottages, from Norman to modern, set amongst mature trees around the green and church. Sutton, once a royal manor, acquired its present name in the 12th century when Henry II gave the village to Reginald de Courtenay. He built Norman Hall about 1190; it still stands across the road from the George and Dragon. South of The Green, partly hidden by trees, lies the gabled and battlemented abbey (1350); originally a country residence for the abbots of Abingdon, it is now a retreat and conference centre. At the opposite end of Church Street is The Wharf (including Walton House), for many years the home of Prime Minister Herbert Asquith until his death in 1928.

ABINGDON A Thames-side town which grew up around the gates of Abingdon Abbey. Founded in 675, the abbey was the sixth richest in Britain and the largest private landowner in Berkshire. All that remains today is the 15th century Gateway, between St Nicholas church and the former St John's Hospital, and a range of domestic buildings along the mill stream including the Granary, Checker (1260) and Long Gallery (1500). (**Appendix C.**)

The grandest free-standing town hall in England dominates Abingdon's Market Place. Known as the County Hall - Abingdon being the county town of Berkshire from 1556 to 1869 - it was built in 1678-82 by Christopher Kempster, one of Wren's master masons. Since that time the roof has proved to be an excellent place from which to throw buns to the populace gathered below - Abingdon's unusual way of celebrating important national events.

From the County Hall, walk down East St Helens - the town's finest street - to St Helen's church where a 13th century spire towers above the second widest church in England. Its greatest glory is a unique, painted wooden ceiling dating from 1391. Surrounding the churchyard are three sets of charming almshouses: Long Alley (1446), Twitty's (1707) and Brick Alley (1718).

WALK 26

Dorchester - Wittenham Clumps
(Walk A 4 miles, Walk B 2 miles)

From Roman Dorchester this walk crosses open country to Day's Lock and then climbs to the top of Wittenham Clumps - one of the finest viewpoints in the Thames valley. A descent via Castle Hill and Little Wittenham Wood is followed by a return path along the riverside.

O.S. Maps:	Landranger 164. Pathfinder 1136.
Start (579,940):	Dorchester Bridge car park (with toilets). $3^1/2$ miles NW of Wallingford on a minor road off the A423.
Terrain:	Walk A: level with one steep climb, five stiles. Walk B: level, two stiles.
Refreshments:	Dorchester: The Fleur de Lys Inn (Free House) 01865-340502 SDA, G, CA, CM, DA. Chesters (Tea-room) 01865-341467 daily, summer 10-5.30, winter 10.30-4.30, DA in courtyard.

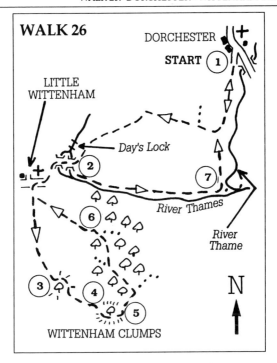

WALK 26

DORCHESTER

START ①

LITTLE
WITTENHAM

Day's Lock

②

⑦

River Thames

River
Thame

N

③ ④ ⑤ ⑥

WITTENHAM CLUMPS

Public Transport: Oxford-Wallingford-Reading 105(RB) M-Sat;
Oxford-Abingdon-Henley 390(T) daily.

Walk A (4 miles)

Route:

1. From DORCHESTER Bridge car park walk down Bridge End to
The Chequers pub. Veer right here and then left down Wittenham
Lane. In 170 yards the lane becomes a footpath running along the
left-hand edge of a field. At the corner, turn right and continue along
the field boundary. Dyke Hills on your left consist of two large
banks and ditches; together with the Rivers Thames and Thame
they once enclosed a 114-acre Iron Age town. After 200 yards go
ahead over a crossing of paths into a fenced bridleway. Soon pass

through a gate into a meadow and take a path going half left towards an arched bridge over the Thames at DAY'S LOCK.

2.   Cross the bridge and two others before climbing a lane into LITTLE WITTENHAM. Opposite the church (open) go through a gate into Little Wittenham Nature Reserve. WITTENHAM CLUMPS lie ahead. Our route continues along the right-hand field edge and then straight up Round Hill. At the summit a topograph helps you to identify features in Oxfordshire and neighbouring Buckinghamshire.

3.   Turn left. Follow a fence contouring the hill. On the opposite side, enjoy more panoramic views before swinging left and descending across open grazing towards the left side of Castle Hill. Aim for a stile surrounded by bushes. On approaching the bushes ignore a path leading off to the left.

4.   Beyond the stile cross Iron Age embankments and ditch to reach a narrow field. Go forwards over the field to a small gap in the trees on top of Castle Hill. Follow a path into the woodland and turn left at a T-junction. A few yards further on, an information plaque is attached to a log on your left. Continue along the path to a dead beech tree at the edge of the wood. This is the Poem Tree on which, in 1844, Joseph Tubb of nearby Warborough Green carved a poem in praise of Wittenham Clumps. Some of the words can still be read. The full text is displayed on a standing stone a few yards away. To the south-east, crowned with a few trees, lies Brightwell Barrow. From the wood take a path leading half left across an open field to reach a stile.

5.   Beyond the stile, descend alongside Little Wittenham Wood. Halfway down, bear left over another stile and enter a broad ride cutting across a woodland valley. Halfway up the far side fork right into the trees. In 300 yards our path arrives at a T-junction with a bridleway. Swing left here to reach a gate into a meadow.

6.   Take a track leading half right across the meadow towards the red brick Manor House, left of Little Wittenham church. At the far side, rejoin the outward route and pass through a gate opposite the church. Turn right. Retrace your steps back across the river. Immediately beyond the final bridge, turn sharply left and walk down to the riverside. Turn left again under the bridge. Our route

now follows the towpath for ³/₄ mile to reach a footbridge over the River Thame.

7.   This is the point at which the Thame joins the Isis (the original and alternative name of the upper Thames) to form the Thame-Isis or Thames. In other words, the true start of the River Thames! Do not cross the footbridge but bear left alongside the River Thame. After 100 yards our path diverges from the river and goes across a field towards a stile (if the stile is impassable, there is a gap in the fence 50 yards left). Continue ahead over the next field, which gradually narrows. Re-cross Dyke Hills and climb a stile in the right-hand field corner to rejoin the outward route. Retrace your steps back to Dorchester.

Walk B (2 miles)

Route:
Follow Instruction 1 of Walk A to reach point 2 on the map. Do not cross the bridge but walk down to the riverside. Turn left under the bridge. Proceed along the towpath for ³/₄ mile to reach a footbridge over the River Thame. Now follow Walk A from Instruction 7.

Points of Interest

DORCHESTER A picturesque High Street winds through the timber framed inns, attractive houses and thatched cottages which make up this charming village, dominated at the southern end by the magnificent Abbey Church. Bought for £140 at the Dissolution (1536), when the abbey itself was destroyed, and given to the village by Richard Beauforest, its sanctuary holds three great traceried windows from the 14th century. The most famous of these, the Jesse window, combines tracery, sculpture and brilliant stained glass in the form of a tree portraying the descent of Christ. It is unique. Originally a Roman town, Dorchester became a centre of Christianity in 635 when Bishop Birinus founded a cathedral here. For a time Dorchester controlled the vast Mercian diocese. In 1140 the Saxon cathedral was replaced by an Augustinian abbey.

DAY'S LOCK A lovely spot in the shadow of Wittenham Clumps and site of the Annual World Poohsticks Championships. Lovers of *Winnie the Pooh* gather here on the first Sunday in January to drop sticks from the arched bridge. Marked in different colours, they float downriver to the winning post. Started in 1984 by former lock keeper Mr Lynn David, proceeds from the event go to the Royal National Lifeboat Institution.

LITTLE WITTENHAM A single street with a few cottages, a manor house and church make up this rural hamlet. The 14th century church of St Peter is unremarkable except for a fine set of alabaster effigies of Mary Dunch (Oliver Cromwell's aunt), her husband Sir William (MP for Wallingford) and their nine children. Immediately west of the church and behind the red brick manor stands a complex of buildings which house the offices, workshops and education centre of Little Wittenham Nature Reserve. Although medieval in appearance, many of the buildings were erected during 1985-95. Especially notable is the replica church tower in golden limestone.

WITTENHAM CLUMPS Comprising tree-topped Round Hill and Castle Hill they form part of the 250-acre Little Wittenham Nature Reserve, which also includes surrounding grassland and Little Wittenham Wood. Woodland in the reserve can be explored by public rights of way and permitted paths while entry to the grassland is unrestricted. Over 100 species of birds and 30 varieties of butterfly have been spotted here. It is also home to 3,000 great crested newts - one of the largest populations in the country. The Iron Age fort on Castle Hill remains unexcavated but pottery finds indicate occupation from 500 BC onwards.

WALK 27

Whitehorse Hill - The Downs

(10 miles)

A classic walk through some of the finest downland scenery in Oxfordshire, including the legendary Whitehorse Hill - highest point in the county, Uffington Castle, Wayland's Smithy, Ashdown House, Alfred's Castle, the Ridgeway path and Ashbury village. Allow yourself plenty of time to enjoy the spectacular views and sites of historic interest.

O.S. Maps:	Landranger 174. Pathfinder 1154.
Start (264,851):	Park and start at Ashbury Methodist church. If coming from the Wantage direction, turn right at the war memorial. 9 miles W of Wantage at a junction of the B4507 and B4000.
Terrain:	Undulating, some long climbs. Five stiles.
Refreshments:	Ashbury: The Rose and Crown Hotel (Arkells) 01793-710222 SDA, G, CA, CM, DA in G. S.
Public Transport:	Swindon-Lambourn 47/A(TD) M-Sat. Swindon-Wantage-Reading X47(T) Sun, Bank Hols, May-Oct.

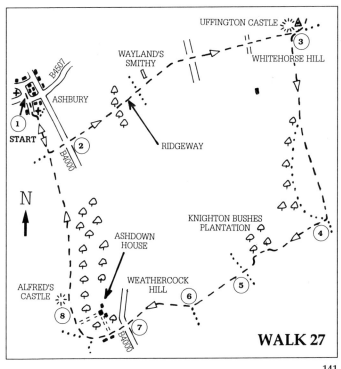

Route:

1.   Walk uphill towards the main road, passing the war memorial on your right. Cross to the far side. Continue uphill on a lane running alongside The Rose and Crown. In 150 yards reach ASHBURY church (open). A tarmac path veers right past a cottage and then left alongside the churchyard wall. When the tarmac path turns right, continue forwards onto a track which soon swings left. Halfway along the back of the churchyard, branch right onto a path ascending between fields. As you climb, look back for a panoramic view over Wiltshire and the Vale of White Horse, with Swindon prominent in the west and the village of Bourton 2¹/₂ miles north-west. After ¹/₂ mile arrive at the Ridgeway (**Appendix A**). Turn left. Although the track is surrounded by tall hedges, sizeable gaps allow good views of the downland scenery. In ¹/₄ mile cross the B4000.

2.   Three-quarters of a mile further on, time can be spent exploring WAYLAND'S SMITHY - a Neolithic long barrow attractively set amongst trees. Our route along the Ridgeway now follows a mostly upward gradient for 1¹/₄ miles towards WHITE HORSE HILL. At the summit, turn left through a small wooden gate and walk to the triangulation point (856ft, 261m). Enjoy stunning panoramic views from the top of Oxfordshire. The impressive 8-acre hill-fort, known as Uffington Castle, is on your left. To see the White Horse itself, continue forwards (i.e. northwards) for a further 200 yards to reach a track running from left to right. Turn right and in 50 yards arrive at the White Horse. Note also Dragon Hill and the Manger. Retrace your steps back to the Ridgeway path.

3.   Turn right. After 80 yards go left onto a signposted bridleway running gently downhill along a field edge. Soon pass Woolstone Hill Barn, ¹/₃ mile off the path to your right. When the field comes to an end, bear left for 30 yards before continuing forwards along a fenced track. At a belt of trees, go through a gap between wooden posts. The bridleway swings right here, but our route goes straight ahead on a footpath ("No Horses") gradually descending for ³/₄ mile across an open field. Kingston Warren Down, with its lovely pattern of fields, hedges and trees, stretches away to your left. Leave the field via a gap between wooden posts to reach a junction of

The Ridgeway and Whitehorse Hill

bridleways. This is the Berkshire/Oxfordshire boundary.

4. Turn right along a bridleway which follows the county boundary down into Whit Coombe and towards a plantation of trees on the valley bottom (Knighton Bushes Plantation). Clumps of snowdrop and daffodil brighten up the plantation in springtime. Beyond the trees our route turns left for 100 yards and then right for a similar distance before reaching a crossing of tracks.

5. Go forwards over the crossing and gradually climb towards Weathercock Hill. Alongside the track and behind bushes on your left can be seen sarsens - large boulders of hard sandstone. Look back from here for good views of Whitehorse Hill. Keep to the main track and ignore paths going right. Stop at a 7ft (2m) standing stone near to the summit; it marks the point at which the main track veers left.

6. Turn a quarter right here (indicated by a footpath sign) and walk across an open field towards the horizon. Two trees with a tall post between them gradually become visible in front of you. Aim for the left-hand tree, passing a clump of bushes 150 yards away to your left. Soon arrive at a stile. ASHDOWN HOUSE can now be

143

seen ahead. Cross into the next field (a Countryside Commission Access Site) and continue in the same direction, going towards a group of farm buildings in the valley below (left of Ashdown House). As you descend, aim for a stile in the far fence.

7. Cross the stile and B4000 road. Maintain course down a private drive to Ashdown Farm, noting the sarsen stones in an adjacent field. On reaching the farm, look right for an excellent view of Ashdown House. One hundred yards beyond the farm buildings, the main drive turns left. Our route continues ahead on a minor track between steel gate posts and curves to the right. After passing through more steel posts, it follows a grassy, ascending path signposted: "Ashbury 2". Halfway to the summit, enjoy a final view of Ashdown House on your right. Climb a stile at the top of the hill to arrive at the Iron Age hill-fort known as Alfred's Castle. Although built about 1,000 years before the time of Alfred, it may well have been his stronghold and close to the spot where he defeated the Danes at the battle of Ashdown in 871.

8. The path continues along the right-hand edge of a field and in 100 yards reaches a stile. Cross the stile and turn half left. Take the path (marked with yellow arrows) running down the middle of a long, narrow field. In $1/3$ mile, come to a fence. Continue alongside the fence for a further $1/3$ mile to a stile. Beyond the stile, follow a track which climbs towards a line of trees on the horizon. These mark the route of the Ridgeway path. Soon cross over the Ridgeway and retrace your outward steps back to Ashbury.

Points of Interest

ASHBURY A remote downland village of thatched chalk cottages, a church dating from Norman times and a fine 15th century manor house - now part of Manor Farm. The first Sunday School in England to be housed outside a church opened here in 1777. Although starting in the church, it soon moved to thatched cottages (now called "Eastwood") opposite the Methodist church. The national Sunday School movement, which grew from this simple beginning, numbered about 200,000 boys by 1786. Besides religion, these first Sunday Schools also taught reading, writing and arithmetic. On the north wall of St Mary's is a memorial to Thomas

Stock, the curate who took this important step towards universal education in England.

WAYLAND'S SMITHY An exceptionally fine 5,000-year old long barrow. Detailed excavations in 1962-3 revealed the presence of three mortuary chambers where more than 20 people had been buried. Always a place of mystery, the "Smithy" is associated with the mythical Saxon smith, Wayland. It is claimed that a horse left here overnight with a silver coin for payment will be re-shod by morning.

WHITEHORSE HILL In 1995 arguments as to whether the famed White Horse - the oldest hill figure in Britain - was of Iron Age or Saxon origin were shown to be irrelevant. In that year a new dating method (Optical Stimulated Luminescence) gave a date of around 1,000 BC, i.e. late Bronze Age, for construction of the White Horse. At the same time excavations at the adjacent hill-fort of Uffington Castle showed it to be of a similar age and in continuous use from the late Bronze Age and throughout the Iron Age and Romano-British periods. In view of this evidence we can reasonably assume that the White Horse was simply the tribal emblem of late Bronze Age occupants of Uffington Castle.

Westwards from Whitehorse Hill the terrain quickly descends into a remarkable dry valley with steep, undulating sides known as The Manger - where the Horse is said to feed. Northwards lies Dragon Hill, a small, flat-topped mound. Legend has it that St George slew the dragon here, the bare patch on the summit being the spot where its blood was spilt.

ASHDOWN HOUSE An unusual house of four storeys. Built of chalk with stone corner blocks, its hipped roof is topped with a cupola and golden ball. Pevsner calls it the "perfect doll's house". The building was constructed about 1660 by the first Lord Craven for Elizabeth, Queen of Bohemia, sister of Charles I. Sadly Elizabeth died of the plague in London before the house was completed. It is now owned by the National Trust and open to the public (**Appendix C**).

WALK 28

The Letcombes - The Ridgeway

(Walk A 4¹/₂ miles, Walk B 3¹/₄ miles)

Nestling beneath the Downs picturesque Letcombe Regis and Letcombe Bassett are home to some of the most successful horse racing stables in the county. Both routes connect the villages via the steep-sided combe of Letcombe Brook; Walk A also incorporates a breezy section of the Ridgeway, affording wide views over rural Oxfordshire and Berkshire.

O.S. Maps:	Landranger 174. Pathfinder 1154.
Start (381,865):	Entrance to Letcombe Regis church. Park on the road north of the church, opposite the back of the village school. 1 mile SW of Wantage on a minor road off the B4507.
Terrain:	Walk A: Gentle inclines, one long climb. Two stiles. Walk B: Gentle inclines. Seven stiles.
Refreshments:	Letcombe Regis: The Greyhound (Morland) 01235-770905 SDA, G, PA, CA, CM, DA.
Public Transport:	From Wantage: 38(T) M-Sat. From Faringdon: 68(TD) W, F. Swindon-Reading X47(T) Sun, Public Hols, May-Oct.

Walk A (4¹/₂ miles)

Route:

1. With your back to the entrance gate of LETCOMBE REGIS church, turn right. Take the footpath alongside the churchyard which veers right past the main entrance and thatched gatehouse of Letcombe Laboratory. Continue alongside school playing fields to reach a second entrance gate. Fine landscaped grounds are visible beyond the gate. Bear right here into a narrow tarmac path. Soon cross Letcombe Brook and arrive at a road. Turn left. Follow the roadside path, enjoying a second view of the Laboratory grounds. After 250 yards, branch left at a footpath sign and enter a lane going

146

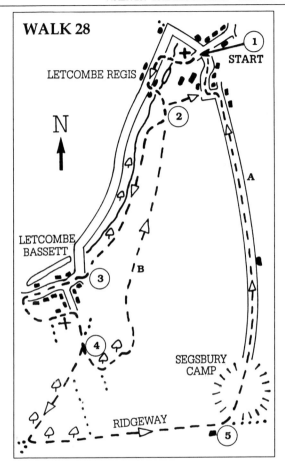

WALK 28

LETCOMBE REGIS

N

LETCOMBE
BASSETT

START

A

B

SEGSBURY
CAMP

RIDGEWAY

1

2

3

4

5

past Ashbrook Barn. Recross Letcombe Brook. The path continues through a gate and straight ahead along the left side of a field. At the far end, exit via another gate into a fenced bridleway. Turn right.

2. In 50 yards turn right again along a narrow fenced path. Letcombe Brook quickly comes into view amongst trees in a steep-sided combe on your right. Our route stays close to the Brook for the

147

next $^1/_2$ mile. On approaching Letcombe Bassett, the old watercress beds - now a wide, empty expanse of water - become visible on the right. Soon join a farm track and come to a road. To view the watercress beds, make a 100 yard detour to the right, otherwise turn left.

3.   Walk uphill into LETCOMBE BASSETT. At a road junction in the village centre, keep going in the same direction towards Childrey. One hundred and fifty yards past the junction, note Arabella's Cottage lying in a hollow next to the old cress beds, on your right. One hundred yards further on, turn left along a footpath between a red brick house and the final barn of Spanswick Farm. (To reach the path, continue past the house before doubling back along a service road). The path quickly enters a field, giving good views of Hackpen Hill and Crowhole Bottom. Keep along the left boundary to reach a stile. Beyond the stile our route continues beside the right-hand edge of the next field and towards a church tower. Leave the field by an iron gate. Follow a lane into the village, passing the church (open) on your right. Bear right at a road junction and walk uphill past thatched cottages. In 200 yards arrive at a footpath sign on your left, labelled: "Circular Walk Ridgeway 1$^3/_4$".

4.   Continue forwards for a further 200 yards to a point where the road divides. Take the right fork up Gramp's Hill. As you climb, digress occasionally through large gaps in the trees on your right and enjoy some superb downland scenery, including the Devil's Punchbowl. Finally come to a crossroads with the Ridgeway (**Appendix A**). Turn left. At first the outlook is restricted by hedges, but after passing a side road, spectacular panoramas open up over the Vale of White Horse on your left and into Berkshire on the right. The track now descends steadily for $^1/_2$ mile to reach the buildings of Segsbury Farm.

5.   Opposite the last barn, branch left onto a farm track signposted: "Public Right of Way". In 100 yards pass through a gap in the embankment of SEGSBURY CAMP. Our path exits the camp in a similar fashion, a $^1/_4$ mile further on. Pause here for a moment to take in the glorious view before plunging down a metalled lane (Warborough Road) towards Letcombe Regis. Follow the road into the village, first turning left at The Sparrow, and then right past

Arabella's Cottage, Letcombe Bassett

delightful thatched cottages (one dated 1680) to reach the starting point.

Walk B (3¹/₄ miles)

Route:

Follow Instructions 1 to 3 of Walk A to reach point 4 on the map. Bear left through a gap in the trees onto the signposted path. Proceed ahead along the right side of a fenced field, past a wooden electricity pole. Enjoy good views over the Oxfordshire Plain as you walk towards a stile in the field corner. Beyond the stile, descend alongside Hell Bottom Copse. In 20 yards, turn left into the copse and soon exit from the far side. Turn right. Keep to the edge of the next field, swinging left at the corner. Halfway along the right-hand field boundary, climb a stile into a fenced farm track. Turn left. We now follow this track for ³/₄ mile, first via a gate, and then along a left-hand field boundary and through a second gate, before rejoining the outward route. Our walk continues ahead for a further 50 yards to arrive at point 2 on the map. Do not turn left here but remain on the bridleway as it veers right. In 200 yards enter a metalled road in Letcombe Regis. Bear left past delightful thatched cottages (one dated 1680) to reach the starting point.

Points of Interest

LETCOMBE REGIS For hundreds of years a Royal manor of the Kings of Wessex and then of England - hence the Regis suffix. These days the village is an attractive blend of white thatched cottages and red brick houses and home to four racehorse stables. In the centre, St Andrew's church boasts a Norman font and fragments of 14th century stained glass in the east window. Letcombe Laboratory, with its splendid Gothic gatehouse, occupies one of the three manor houses in the village. It is owned by the international company Dow Elanco, who test fungicides here. The story is told that a previous owner objected to the presence of naked statues in the grounds and had them thrown into the lake. On dredging the lake in 1982, a second century marble statue of Hercules was recovered. It subsequently sold for £28,000!

LETCOMBE BASSETT A small community of thatched cottages beneath the Downs. The name derives from "lede in the combe" i.e. brook in the valley; Bassett was added in the 12th century when one Richard Bassett held the manor. Thomas Hardy called it "Cresscombe" in his tragic novel *Jude the Obscure*, recognising Letcombe Bassett's reputation for growing watercress. Shouts of "Bassett cress" once attracted customers in the markets of London. A thatched cottage (Arabella's Cottage) beside the old cress beds is probably the place Hardy had in mind when he described the first meeting of Jude with his future wife, Arabella. Nowadays the training of racehorses has replaced watercress growing as an important local industry.

SEGSBURY CAMP An Iron Age fort of 26 acres defended by a single embankment and ditch. The camp and surrounding fields comprise a Countryside Commission Access Site. Entry is by means of stiles; two are located in the camp centre and two at the northern end. The area is being managed to encourage growth of increasingly rare chalkland grasses and wild flowers.

WALK 29

Ardington - East Hendred

(5¹/₂ miles)

A string of prehistoric villages follows the "spring-line" across the Downs. This walk visits two of the most attractive: Ardington - Lord Wantage's model village - and East Hendred - a picturesque village with many thatched and timber-framed dwellings. Our outward route keeps to the primordial Icknield Way, offering extensive views across the Vale of White Horse.

O.S. Maps:	Landranger 174. Pathfinder 1155.
Start (432,885):	Park and start at the post office, Ardington High Street. 2 miles E of Wantage on a minor road off the A417.
Terrain:	Undulating; one short, steep climb. Five stiles.
Refreshments:	Ardington: P.O./Cobweb Tearooms 01235-833237 daily, inc. Bank Hols; closed Th afternoon. The Boar's Head (Free House) 01235-833254 CA, no food M evening. S. East Hendred: The Wheatsheaf (Morland) 01235-833229 SDA, G, CA, DA in G. The Plough (Morland) 01235-833213 G, PA, CA, CM. S.
Public Transport:	To Ardington, East and West Hendred: 32/A, 35/A, 36/A (T) from Oxford, Abingdon, Didcot, Wantage, Grove, daily.

Route:

1.   With your back to ARDINGTON post office turn left and walk a few yards to a road junction. Swing right along Church Street. Note Ardington House, set back from the road on your left, and pass The Boar's Head Inn and church (closed but key available from the post office). Bear left at the next road junction. An unusual gravestone in the churchyard, depicting an angel and three children, is a memorial to Lord Wantage and his family. Proceed downhill and

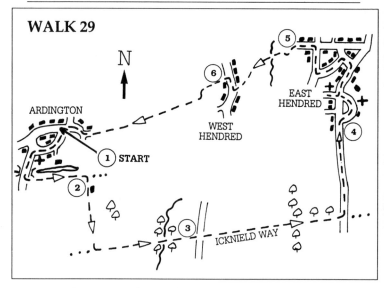

WALK 29

N

ARDINGTON

① START

②

③ ICKNIELD WAY

⑥

WEST
HENDRED

⑤

EAST
HENDRED

④

cross Ardington Brook. In 20 yards, turn left onto a broad, grassy track. This runs alongside a wood and a narrow lake stocked with trout. Further on, a good view of Ardington House opens up between trees on the left. After 1/3 mile enter a farm track and swing right.

2.   The track gradually climbs uphill, passing farm buildings and wooded Roundabout Hill. In 1/2 mile go through a gate into ICKNIELD WAY. Turn left. Our route now follows this broad, grassy track for 11/2 miles, as it winds its way across a gently rolling landscape. After 1/3 mile cross a farm track and descend into the wooded valley of Ginge Brook. The path passes over a bridge before climbing a steep bank. Proceed ahead along the right-hand edge of the next field, noting the stark, symmetrical outline of Goldbury Hill on your left.

3.   At the field end, cross a metalled road and continue along the Way (signposted "Right of Way"). On this section there are good views of the Vale of White Horse to your left. After passing the start of a permissive path to West Hendred (1 mile left), walk down a

Ardington House

right-hand field edge towards a plantation of conifers. Go through the trees and maintain course alongside more conifers. In ¹/₂ mile reach a metalled road. Turn left and walk downhill into EAST HENDRED.

4.   Our route through the village visits some of the most historic buildings and prettiest streets. Beyond a delightful row of cottages, bear right down St Mary's Road. Just past St Mary's church, glance through trees on your right to see the 13th century chapel of St Amand, at the rear of Hendred House. Continue ahead across Newbury Road/High Street into Church Street. The parish church is open and there are some charming cottages beyond it. On returning to the High Street, turn left. As you ascend, note the avenue of trees leading to Hendred House and a superb, early Tudor building occupied by the village shop and post office. Soon swing left into Chapel Square. The 15th century Champs Chapel and adjoining priest's house were built by Carthusian monks. The chapel now houses a museum. Just beyond The Wheatsheaf we go left into Cats Lane and in 300 yards arrive at a T-junction. Turn right here along Ford Lane. One hundred yards further on, the route

branches left into Mill Lane. After passing a recreation ground, bear left onto a narrow, signposted path next to a thatched cottage.

5.   Our track now curves around the cottage, follows a driveway and then goes between trees to reach a bridge over a stream. Beyond the bridge, walk ahead across a narrow field. Proceed over a second bridge and enter a larger field. Turn three-quarters left. Aim 25 yards right of an electricity pole and head towards a short length of wooden fence in the corner of a hedge. Climb a stile in the fence. Follow a left-hand field edge towards a row of houses. At the field end, cross two stiles into a lane. Turn left. After 50 yards swing right along a metalled road leading into West Hendred. In 200 yards the route bears right at a T-junction and goes uphill between houses for 150 yards, before branching left onto a signposted footpath ("Ardington 1").

6.   At first, our path is alongside garden fences but it soon strikes out across an open field. On the far side, turn left at a T-junction with a farm track. After 25 yards, swing right and follow a left-hand field boundary to a hedge. Go through a gap and over a ditch and stile. The path now crosses four fields separated by tall trees / hedges and a single stile. Eventually pass through a gate into a farm track and proceed ahead. In 350 yards enter Ardington. Turn right at a T-junction with a metalled road and soon reach the High Street.

Points of Interest

ARDINGTON Along with its twin village of Lockinge, Ardington formed the centre of a 20,000 acre estate owned by Robert Lloyd-Lindsay (later Lord Wantage) in the 19th century. Together with his wife, he rebuilt and restored the buildings to form a Victorian-Tudor model village for estate workers. Ardington today is a thriving community with many local industries including a pottery, fishery and water mill. An impressive double staircase rising from the grand hall is a notable feature of Ardington House - an early Georgian building in the village centre (**Appendix C**).

ICKNIELD WAY An ancient trackway starting in Norfolk and running westwards to cross the Thames at Goring. West of Goring the route runs parallel to, but at a lower level than, the Ridgeway. It came into use later than the high level track, at a time when valleys had been partially cleared of forest and the wild animal population reduced. Following the spring-line across the Downs, Icknield Way proved popular with travellers and drovers, having abundant water supplies and connecting many villages. The section running eastwards from Goring follows the lower Chiltern slopes to the county boundary. Sometimes it divides into an Upper and Lower Way - the higher route being used in winter when the lower one was waterlogged. Parts of Icknield Way are now incorporated into the road network and the Ridgeway long-distance path (**Appendix A**).

EAST HENDRED One of the most beautiful villages in the county. The many fine dwellings built here by cloth and wool merchants in the 15th and 16th centuries are a reflection of the prosperity which existed before the trade was lost to neighbouring Wantage.

For over 500 years Hendred House has been home to the Eyston family - descendants of Sir Thomas More (Chancellor to Henry VIII). Attached to the house is St Amand's chapel - a place of Catholic worship since 1291.

At 3-hourly intervals, "The Angel's Song" rings out across the village. The hymn tune is played by one of the oldest clocks in England - John Seymour's faceless clock (1525), housed in the parish church. Also worthy of note inside St Augustine's are a pair of beautifully carved, 13th century nave arcades, a unique wooden lectern of a similar age with a base composed of a Crusader's foot trampling three heads of a dragon, and a richly carved octagonal Jacobean pulpit displaying a portrait of Charles I on its front.

WALK 30
Blewbury - Lowbury Hill
(6¹/₂ miles)

This walk, more than any other, brings out the contrast between the vast open spaces of the Downs and the cosy warmth of villages at their feet. Heading south from Blewbury, our path ascends across an undulating landscape towards the top of Lowbury Hill - a place of exhilarating views. Allow yourself extra time to explore the maze of lanes, footpaths, streams and cottages which make up captivating Blewbury.

O.S. Maps:	Landranger 174. Pathfinder 1155.
Start (528,856):	Start and park in Westbrook Street, Blewbury. Westbrook Street is the first turning left off the A417 when entering Blewbury from the west. 2 miles S of Didcot.
Terrain:	Easy inclines, some lengthy. Five stiles.
Refreshments:	Blewbury: The Red Lion (Brakspear) 01235-850403 two SDAs, G, CA in non-smoking SDA, CM, DA in G, M-F 11-2.30, 6-11, Sat 11-11, Sun 12-10.30. Lantern Cottage Tearoom, South Street, Sun afternoons in summer.
Public Transport:	From Didcot: C(C), F.

Route:

1.   From Westbrook Street walk back to the A417 and turn left. After 250 yards reach a small war memorial at the entrance to Nottingham Fee. Cross the A417 here. Take a signposted footpath between houses, ignoring a path which soon goes off to the right. Continue ahead, gradually climbing a sunken track between hedges and fences. In 300 yards pass Blewbury Reservoir. Pause occasionally to turn round and admire the widening view. Blewburton Hill (an Iron Age hill-fort to the east of Blewbury), Wittenham Clumps, the Chilterns and Didcot power station quickly become visible. Shortly beyond a wooded valley running away to the left, the path enters an open area of hawthorn bushes and unfenced fields. Note a small conifer plantation across a field on your right. A short distance beyond the plantation is Churn Knob (not visible) - the place where St Birinus first preached to the people of Wessex in 634. A pilgrimage takes place between here and Dorchester Abbey each July to commemorate the event.

2.   Continue forwards on a hedge-lined track, slowly descending towards the buildings of Upper Chance Farm. Before reaching the farm, and 50 yards short of a clump of conifers, turn half right. Our route now follows a broad, grassy, downhill track along the right-

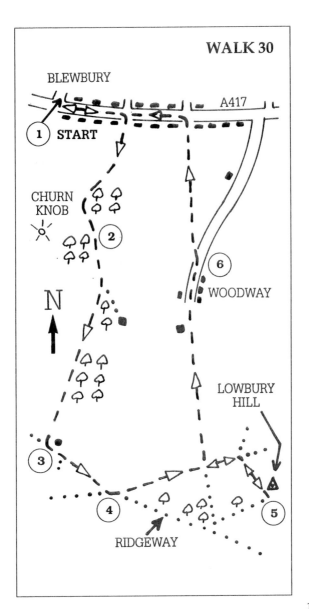

WALK 30

BLEWBURY

A417

(1) START

CHURN KNOB

(2)

N

(6)

WOODWAY

LOWBURY HILL

(3)

(4)

(5)

RIDGEWAY

hand edge of a second group of conifers. This is a delightful area with open fields stretching away to the distant horizon. When the plantation comes to an end, do not continue along the track as it veers slightly left, but keep going in the same direction. Follow a path along the left-hand edge of a field, aiming 50 yards to the right of a small brick building in the distance. As you walk, note two burial mounds (probably Bronze Age) in the field on your right. On approaching the building, pass a footpath sign ("Blewbury 2") and cross a concrete road to arrive at a T-junction with a grassy track. Turn left.

3.   The brick bridge across the field to your right is a remnant of the railway line which once ran between Didcot and Southampton. Churn Halt station lay a short distance right of the bridge. Follow the track, gradually climbing uphill between hawthorn trees. In $^1/_2$ mile reach a T-junction with the Ridgeway path (**Appendix A**) and bear left.

4.   After 150 yards branch a quarter left off the Ridgeway onto a signposted "Public Right of Way". Half a mile along this path come to a crossing of tracks. Here, a broad grassy track leads leftwards towards a barn on the skyline (our return route); at the same time, a path to the right heads for a small conifer plantation. Maintain course for a further 300 yards to arrive at a path veering off to the left, marked by a blue arrow. The field on your right here is a Countryside Commission access site (indicated by a green noticeboard). Turn three-quarters right and climb across this field to a stile in the far left-hand corner. You are now at the highest point reachable by rights of way and the Access Site. Although not visible, the triangulation point is situated in the field ahead, about 100 yards half left from the stile. On a clear day the views from LOWBURY HILL (611ft, 186m) extend for 20-30 miles.

5.   Retrace your steps to the crossing of tracks, passed earlier. Turn right here onto the grassy track leading towards a barn on the horizon. In 1 mile come to the hamlet of Woodway.

6.   One hundred yards beyond the last building, climb a bank on your left and cross a stile. The stile is set back 15 yards from the lane and partially hidden by a hedge. Our route now descends across four fields and between houses to reach the A417 in BLEWBURY.

Turn left. Soon rejoin the outward route and return to the starting point.

Points of Interest

LOWBURY HILL Evidence suggests that an enclosed Roman settlement existed here from about 200-400 AD; it was either a temple or farm, comprising two wooden buildings with tiled roofs. Scattered around the site are fragments of oyster shells and pottery left by the inhabitants. The O.S. triangulation point has a memorial plaque to Peter Sowden MBE 1944-1991, Field Survey Instructor, School of Military Survey.

BLEWBURY A spring-line village having the finest set of cob walls in Oxfordshire. Constructed of chalky mud and straw topped with thatch, these attractive features have probably come down from Saxon times. For the last 150 years Blewbury has been a magnet for artists and writers. Kenneth Grahame of *Wind in the Willows* fame lived here between 1910 and 1924.

The village can only be properly explored on foot. From our starting point in Westbrook Street, walk away from the A417. In 350 yards arrive at Grahame Close on the right-hand side, built in the grounds of Bohams House - Grahame's old home. Turn right onto a footpath beside the close. Pass a cob wall. Beyond a stream, enter a small green with a crossing of paths - the village "hub". Turn left to visit the church. Miserly Morgan Jones, the curate here from 1781 to 1824, lived on $12^{1/2}$ pence a week and wore the same black coat for 42 years. Dickens mentions him ("Blewbury Jones") in *Our Mutual Friend*. Nearby is the School House (1709) built by money left by William Malthus for the education of poor children. Go forwards from the "hub" to see the eastern side of the village; or turn right between cob walls to reach The Red Lion, Chapel Lane, Watery Lane and Nottingham Fee.

WALK 31
Goring - River Thames
(4¹/₂ miles)

At Goring Gap the Thames cuts through the great chalk ridge running across southern Oxfordshire. Starting from the attractive village of Goring-on-Thames this walk explores the beautiful contryside around the Gap - from thickly wooded hillsides offering distant views, to pleasant paths beside the river.

O.S. Maps:	Landranger 174, 175. Pathfinder 1155, 1156, 1171, 1172.
Start (599,807):	Park and start at the central car park (with toilets) in Goring. 6 miles S of Wallingford on the B4009.
Terrain:	Gentle inclines; one lengthy climb. Ten stiles.
Refreshments:	Goring: The Catherine Wheel (Brakspear) 01491-872379 SDA, G, CA, DA in G and bar, no food Sun evening. Riverside Tearoom, daily, summer 10-6, winter 10-5. S.
Public Transport:	Rail: From Reading, Didcot, Oxford, Banbury (TT) daily. Bus: Swindon-Reading X47(T) Sun, Bank Hols, May-Oct.

Route:

1.   From the car park walk past the toilets to reach GORING High Street. Turn right here. Our path soon crosses a railway bridge and comes to a T-junction. Turn right again. After 100 yards bear left along the B4526. Take the second turning right (Whitehills Green) into a housing estate and follow the road round to the left. When the road terminates at a traffic island, we swing right along a narrow path between hedges to arrive at a stile and footpath sign. A recreation ground lies ahead. Go straight across, aiming for a stile hidden in a hedge, 50 yards right of the far left-hand corner. Beyond

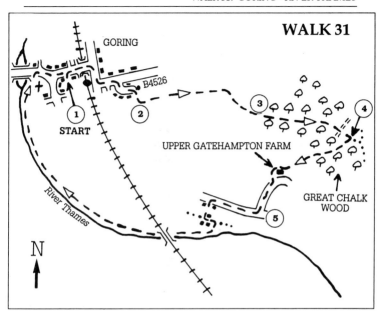

WALK 31

GORING

B4526

① START

②

③

④

UPPER GATEHAMPTON FARM

River Thames

GREAT CHALK WOOD

⑤

N

the stile, turn left and follow the field edge uphill.

2.   For the next ¹/₄ mile our path continues to ascend; first through a gap in a hedge, and then along the left boundary of another field to a stile at the distant end. As you climb, it is worthwhile looking back occasionally for an ever widening view over the Thames valley and North Wessex Downs. The track keeps to the left edge of the next field, gently falling and curving right into a valley. At the far side, cross a stile and proceed between tall bushes.

3.   In 50 yards, negotiate a second stile to enter the Great Chalk Wood. Our ascending route is indicated by yellow arrows on white discs and on the trees. Ignore all side tracks. After ¹/₃ mile the path levels out and starts to descend, soon reaching a major crossroads - identified by a wide road dropping out of the woods on your left. Continue ahead from here. Eighty yards further on, just before the track veers left and descends more steeply, turn sharply right onto

a wide path going gently uphill.

4.   Follow the main track as it gradually veers right. In 300 yards cross a stile at the edge of the wood to enter a field. Go straight across, aiming for the middle of a row of buildings ahead (Upper Gatehampton Farm). On the far side walk between parked vehicles and bear right along a gravelled track. After the last farm building, proceed forwards past the end of more vehicles. Immediately swing left, passing the backs of the vehicles and a mound of earth. Do not enter adjacent fields. In 25 yards reach an unobtrusive stile at the bottom of a garden belonging to a white farmhouse. Beyond the stile our route follows a fenced path to another stile and then goes across two narrow, grassy paddocks before arriving at a metalled lane. Turn right here. The lane descends between trees and hedges to a T-junction.

5.   There is a wide gap in the hedge at this point, giving good views across the Thames to Lower Basildon and the well-wooded National Trust property of Basildon Park. Turn right. In $^1/_3$ mile pass Gatehampton House. In a further 50 yards, swing left between houses onto a broad, downhill track. We soon come to a T-junction with a bridleway (signposted "Whitchurch $2^1/_2$"). Bear left here, alongside Gattendon Lodge. After 80 yards take a fenced path branching off to the right and leading down to the Thames. On reaching the towpath turn right and enjoy a pleasant, $1^1/_2$ mile stroll back to Goring Bridge and Lock. Swing right at the bridge and follow the High Street back towards the car park.

Points of Interest

GORING A prosperous village of red brick and flint. Prehistoric Icknield Way (**Walk 29**) crosses the river here. To meet the needs of travellers, settlements grew up on either bank - Goring on the east side and Streatley on the west. Until the first bridge was built in 1837, the villages were connected by ferry. This means of conveyance was not without its problems for, in 1674, a boat returning to Streatley from Goring Fair overturned and some 40 people lost their lives. The present bridge dates from 1923. In the village centre, a typically Norman church houses one of the oldest bells in England, cast in 1290. No longer rung, it now hangs above the west door. The fine Rood Screen (1920) is fashioned of oak from HMS *Thunderer* - a bomb-ketch which served under Nelson at Trafalgar.

WALK 32
Nuffield - Ipsden
(7³/₄ miles)

From Nuffield, a high point in the southern Chilterns, our walk first drops down beside the wooded earthworks of Grim's Ditch before swinging south along the Icknield Way to Ipsden. After exploring this scattered settlement, you can be suitably refreshed at a pub with the finest view in Oxfordshire! Pleasant paths join with magnificent panoramas to make this an enjoyable walk at all times of the year.

O.S. Maps:	Landranger 175. Pathfinder 1156.
Start (668,874):	Park and start at Nuffield church. 5 miles E of Wallingford on a minor road off the A4130.
Terrain:	A gradual descent followed by a similar ascent. Eleven stiles.
Refreshments:	Hailey: King William IV (Brakspear) 01491-680675 SDA, G, CA, DA in G. Nuffield: The Crown (Brakspear) 01491-641335 SDA, G, CA in SDA (lunchtime only), DA except for large wet ones!
Public Transport:	To Nuffield (The Crown): Oxford-Abingdon-Henley 390(T) daily. To reach the starting point you need to follow the Ridgeway path for ¹/₂ mile. Walk downhill from The Crown past a phone box. Go along a gravel drive. Pass Fairway Cottage and then follow seven white posts over a golf course to Nuffield church.

Route:

1.   Before setting out it is worthwhile having a look at NUFFIELD church. The first 2¹/₄ miles of our route follow the Ridgeway path.

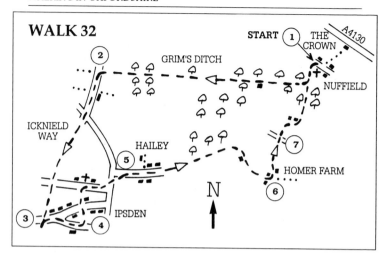

From the church walk downhill for 50 yards to a Ridgeway sign. Turn left. The path keeps to the left edge of a field, providing extensive views across the Thames valley to the North Wessex Downs, with Didcot power station dominating the middle ground. Go through a kissing gate at the field boundary. Descend through trees and in 130 yards reach the earthworks of GRIM'S DITCH. Bear right here. For the next 2 miles our route continues on a downwards gradient alongside the ditch. For most of the way, the path is shaded by trees; where these are absent, you can enjoy more fine views. Several kissing gates, stiles and a bluebell wood (Oaken Copse) are passed before coming to a quiet metalled road - the ICKNIELD WAY (see **Walk 29**).

2.   Turn left. Our path follows the ancient route for $1^{3/4}$ miles. In $^{1/2}$ mile go forwards over crossroads onto a wide, grassy bridleway. This soon becomes a narrow path running along a delightful valley - quaintly named Drunken Bottom. Coblers Hill is on your right. After $^{3/4}$ mile cross a road and continue along a fenced bridleway. In a further $^{1/2}$ mile arrive at a second road.

3.   You are now on the outskirts of IPSDEN. Cross the road and follow a path to the far end of a copse. The Reade Memorial stands

in the trees on your right. Return to the road, bear right, and soon enter the village. Note the huge red-brick barn of Ipsden Farm on your left - reputedly the largest in Oxfordshire. Opposite is an old grain store; it is mounted on stone mushrooms to keep the rats out. The road divides here. Take the right fork past thatched cottages and gradually climb uphill. In 200 yards reach Ipsden House, home of the Reade family. After a further 200 yards branch left onto a signposted path running alongside a cricket field.

4. Soon pass a small circle of stones. Continue ahead, descending along a field edge to reach a road. Maintain course over the road and up a wide grassy track. Follow this track to the village war memorial - a monument commanding beautiful views of the surrounding countryside. Beyond the memorial, cross a road to look at the village well and church. On leaving, swing left along the road. In 200 yards turn half left onto a short path cutting across the corners of two fields and passing over a road and four stiles on the way.

5. At the final stile, turn right into a lane and enter the hamlet of Hailey. Our route now proceeds uphill, past the pub with a view. The lane soon becomes a farm track. It is worthwhile looking back occasionally to admire an ever widening panorama. The walk continues through Bixmoor Wood, following the main track all the way. When the trees come to an end, pass entrances to Fudgers Wood on your right, and Homer Farm on the left. One hundred yards further on (at the end of The Old Farm House), turn left through a pair of steel gates onto a signposted footpath ("Nuffield $1^{1}/_{2}$").

6. Go up a farm track for 20 yards. When the track veers left to a workshop, continue straight ahead. Pass a statue on your left and walk across the front of Homer Farm House. Continue forwards through a gap between wooden sheds to reach a stile. Beyond the stile our route carries on in the same direction, following a line of electricity poles across a wide field. Exit from the far side via a stile, 20 yards left of the electricity lines. Cross a narrow field and the entrance drive to Upper House Farm.

7. Ahead, the path we take runs along the left edge of a field towards two buildings. It eventually curves right and follows a fence to reach a stile. Go over the stile. Cross a drive and enter a

fenced path which turns left. Continue on a well-trodden path along a field boundary, through trees, and over a stile (or steps). Follow the right-hand side of the next field. Enter a narrow belt of trees and soon cross the final stile to rejoin our outward path at Grim's Ditch. Retrace your steps back to Nuffield church.

Points of Interest

NUFFIELD The small flint church dating from Norman times boasts a font of similar age with a Latin inscription in Lombardic letters; a later brass to Benert Engliss (1360) is hidden by a mat below the pulpit. In the churchyard, near to a water tap on the west tower, lies the simple grave of William Morris, later Lord Nuffield, who founded the motor works at Cowley which are now part of the Rover group. For many years he lived at Nuffield Place, near to The Crown. A generous benefactor, Morris gave away most of his fortune to hospitals and colleges in Oxford and elsewhere. Nuffield College in Oxford bears his name.

GRIM'S DITCH In addition to the present walk, earthworks of this name are also seen on **Walks 11** and **36**. Their purpose is uncertain but they probably marked the territorial boundaries of Iron Age tribes.

IPSDEN Home of the Reade family since the 16th century. The Victorian novelist Charles Reade, famous for his classic *Cloister and the Hearth*, was born here in 1814. Thirteen years later a most unusual event took place in the village. At that time a member of the family, John Reade, lived in India. His mother often walked down from Ipsden House to meet mail deliveries along the Wallingford Road, hoping to receive a letter from her son. One evening on her way to meet the coach, she saw a ghost of John walking towards her. Shortly afterwards news arrived that he had died of dysentery. The Reade Memorial erected by Edward Reade, supposedly to "lay the ghost of his brother to rest", stands on the very spot where the apparition appeared. Although not so ornate as the Maharajah's Well at Stoke Row (**Walk 35**), Ipsden well - built by another Indian Rajah, Sir Deonarayun Sing in 1865 - is of a similar depth to its more famous twin. It was in use until the 1950s.

WALK 33

Watlington - Christmas Common

(4$^{1}/_{2}$ miles)

Although relatively short, this is a walk of considerable variety. Starting from the attractive medieval town of Watlington our route climbs to the top of Watlington Hill, one of the finest vantage points in the Chilterns. The ensuing path through majestic beech woods is delightful at any season but especially so in spring and autumn.

O.S. Maps:	Landranger 175. Pathfinder 1137.
Start (691,944):	Watlington, Hill Road car park. 6 miles NE of Wallingford on the B4009.
Terrain:	One steep climb and descent. Two stiles.
Refreshments:	Watlington: The Carriers Arms (Free House) 01491-613470 SDA and restaurant, G, PA, CA, DA in bar and G, M-Sat 11-11, Sun 11-4, 7-10.30. Hampden House Tearoom, Couching Street, Sat, Sun afternoons.
Public Transport:	From Oxford: 101(T) M-Sat, except Public Hols. Henley-Thame: 122, 123, 124(RR) Tu, Th, Sat.

Route:

1.   From the car park, walk into Hill Road and turn right. Keep to the roadside pavement as it climbs towards the Chilterns. Beyond a hospital entrance, the White Mark of WATLINGTON, a large triangle, becomes visible on the hillside ahead. In 300 yards arrive at a crossroads with the Icknield Way/Ridgeway path - indicated by a wooden sign on the left and a gravel track on your right.

2.   Continue ahead. After passing house No. 92 the pavement becomes a grassy path which veers right into woodland. A National Trust sign reveals that you are now climbing Watlington Hill. Go forwards for 100 yards to a stile (ignoring one 20 yards earlier on your right). On the far side, enter a region of scrub. Soon come to the

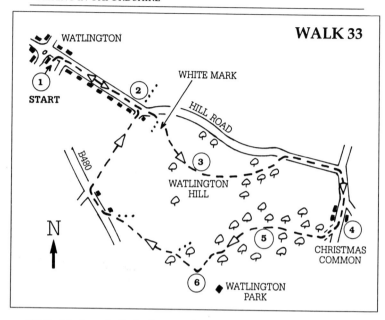

WALK 33

WATLINGTON

WHITE MARK

HILL ROAD

(1)

(2)

START

B480

N

(3)

WATLINGTON
HILL

(5)

(4)

CHRISTMAS
COMMON

(6) ◆ WATLINGTON
PARK

White Mark and climb along its left-hand side. The path proceeds upwards for a further ¹/₄ mile to reach the summit. Here you can enjoy a truly panoramic view. To the north-west, the Oxfordshire Plain stretches out beyond Watlington to a distant horizon. Pyrton and Shirburn Hills dominate the northward scene, while Didcot Power Station, Wittenham Clumps and Swyncombe Downs are visible in the south-west.

3.　From the summit continue ahead on the same path between gorse and hawthorn bushes. Bear slightly left, aiming towards a radio mast on the horizon. Our route, level at first, soon descends along a broad, grassy pathway which eventually narrows to become a tree-flanked track. At the end go through a kissing gate and re-enter Hill Road. Turn right. Follow the roadside path uphill through the National Trust car park and along a grass verge. In ¹/₃ mile turn right at a T-junction. After a further 200 yards take a right-hand fork to reach the hamlet of CHRISTMAS COMMON.

4. When the houses come to an end, bear half right at a footpath sign. Join a metalled drive passing through iron gates set in a brick wall. In 150 yards turn half right onto a woodland path marked with white arrows. Here, ancient oak and beech are interplanted with younger trees and bluebells carpet the woodland glades in springtime. The route gradually descends, soon entering Lower Deans Wood, as indicated by a National Trust sign.

5. After a further $1/4$ mile, the path comes close to the edge of the wood and follows a field boundary behind a screen of trees. Each February, a profusion of snowdrops enlivens this corner of the woodland. When the track crosses a clearing, part of the red-brick, Georgian house of Watlington Park comes into sight on your left, and more splendid views open up to the right. The house was built for John Tilson in 1755. Re-enter the woodland and after 15 yards turn right.

6. Climb a stile and descend across a field to a gate at the bottom. Follow a farm track for 50 yards before joining a well-used track coming in from the right. Continue straight ahead between hedges and fields. Ignore side tracks and in $1/3$ mile enter the B480 road. Turn right. After 300 yards turn right again at Icknield House onto the ancient ICKNIELD WAY (**Walk 29**). In 100 yards a gap in the hedge on your right gives a full, though distant, view of the mansion in Watlington Park. Follow the Icknield Way for a further $1/2$ mile to reach Hill Road. Bear left here and return to the starting point.

Points of Interest

WATLINGTON A fine town hall and interesting houses grace this medieval market town. The mellowed brick town hall, built by Thomas Stonor in 1665 to accommodate a covered market and grammar school, is enlightened by a sundial, clock and weather vane beautifully refurbished in gold, blue and black. Although the modern town radiates outwards from here, the medieval settlement is clustered around St Leonard's church. A short walk through the most picturesque streets can be extended to reach the building.

From the town hall make your way down the High Street, enjoying a wide range of buildings, many Georgian. At the war memorial turn right into Chapel Street. Pass 16th and 17th century cottages and bear left at White Cottage into New Road. At the far end, you can swing left to rejoin the High Street or turn right to view the church, 300 yards distant. St Leonard's is kept locked but a key can be obtained nearby. Apart from a battlemented, 15th century tower, the building was largely rebuilt in 1877. In 1764, dissatisfied with the absence of a spire, Edward Horne had the shape of one cut into the chalk of Watlington Hill, so that from his window the church tower appeared to be topped by a soaring steeple. Hence the White Mark of Watlington!

CHRISTMAS COMMON A hamlet of red brick and flint whose unusual name appears to originate from the Civil War. The story goes that in 1643 Royalists and Roundheads, encamped on opposite sides of the common, called a temporary halt in hostilities to allow the normal celebrations to go ahead on Christmas Day.

WALK 34

Middle Assendon - Stonor

(8 miles)

Some of the best scenery in south Oxfordshire can be enjoyed from this walk. A steady climb up the Assendon valley reveals an ever widening panorama of the glorious Chiltern landscape. We continue past Stonor House - superbly set in its own deer park - before returning through the lovely Bix valley.

O.S. Maps:	Landranger 175. Pathfinder 1156.
Start (739,856):	Park and start at a lay-by 150 yards south of The Rainbow Inn, Middle Assendon. 2¹/₂ miles NW of Henley on the B480.
Terrain:	Two long climbs and descents. Eight stiles.
Refreshments:	Middle Assendon: The Rainbow Inn (Brakspear) 01491-574879 G, CA in G, DA. Stonor: The Stonor Arms (Private Hotel and Restaurant) 01491-638345 SDA, G, CA, DA in G.
Public Transport:	Henley-Thame 122, 123, 124(RR) Tu, Th, Sat. To

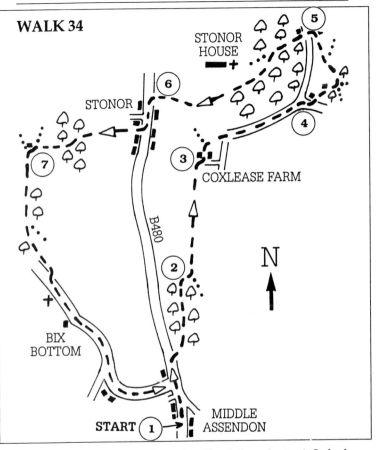

WALK 34

Lower Assendon (³/₄ mile from the start): Oxford-Abingdon-Henley, 390(T) daily.

Route:

1. Walk northwards along the B480, passing The Rainbow Inn and a side-road leading to Bix Bottom. Two hundred yards further on, turn half right onto a track ascending across a field towards a wood. At the trees, look back for a good view of the valley before

bearing left into Paradise Wood. Follow a well-trodden path through the wood and over a stile at the far end.

2.   The path continues uphill along the left-hand edge of a field. After 100 yards swing left. Keep next to the fence and in a further 100 yards bear left again onto a farm track. For the next ³/₄ mile our path gradually climbs towards Coxlease Farm, providing an ever changing platform from which to enjoy the Chiltern landscape.

3.   Follow the track as it veers right past Coxlease Farmhouse. At the far end of a tall yew hedge, turn left into a wide gap between barns. In 100 yards the route divides. Take the right fork alongside a wood. Do not enter the woodland, but follow the path as it curves right around a field to reach the corner of a metalled lane. Walk ahead on a grass verge beside the lane, soon shaded by trees of Kildridge Wood. After ¹/₂ mile arrive at a road junction. Maintain course here on the road signposted to Henley.

4.   In 100 yards, branch left onto a bridleway. The route now passes a duck pond and Kimble Farm before coming to Kimble Wood. As you enter the wood, turn left onto an uphill path beside a wire fence. The path exits the woodland via a stile and continues along the left edge of a field. Near the field end, cross a stile in the fence on your left and immediately turn right. Follow the right-hand field boundary around a fenced hollow filled with trees to arrive at another stile. Cross this and turn left. Proceed along the left side of the next field towards a stile and gate. Beyond the stile go forwards on an unmade drive next to a wood and soon come to a metalled road.

5.   Walk straight across (past house No. 41) onto a wide track descending into Kildridge Wood. For the next 1¹/₄ miles our route is marked by white arrows painted on trees. In 200 yards go forwards over a crossing of tracks and continue dropping through woodland. After a further 300 yards, the track divides. Take the left fork, which gradually climbs through trees to enter STONOR PARK via a turnstile. The right of way through this attractive parkland provides excellent views of Stonor House and perhaps a glimpse of the herd of fallow deer. Leave the park by a turnstile at the B480 road.

Stonor House

6.   Bear left here and walk into Stonor village. After ¹/₄ mile take a footpath between houses on your right, signposted "Maidensgrove 1". Soon negotiate a stile and go forwards on an upward gradient across a field. Climb a second stile. Keep ascending in the same direction over the next field, passing a fenced copse on your left. Aim for a white noticeboard in trees at the field summit. Before entering woodland, look back for a good view of Stonor House. Our path now traverses Park Wood and crosses a field to reach the Oxfordshire Way (**Appendix A**). Swing left along the track between two houses. Bear right at an Oxfordshire Way sign. Go through an iron gate and in 20 yards turn left onto a farm track descending through woods (part of the Warburg Nature Reserve).

7.   For the next 3 miles our path follows the Oxfordshire Way back to Middle Assendon. After ¹/₃ mile the track divides. Take the right fork plunging downhill into woodland. The trees eventually give way to lovely views over the Bix valley. Three hundred yards beyond the wood, turn left at a T-junction with a metalled lane (signposted "Oxfordshire Cycleway"). This single-track road winds its way past the ruined Norman church of St James - abandoned in 1875 for a new building in Bix village, 1 mile south. It then continues

through Bix Bottom to reach the B480. Turn right here and retrace your steps to the starting point.

Points of Interest

STONOR PARK A staunch Roman Catholic family with a distinguished history, the Stonors have lived here since the 12th century. A Stonor led the left wing of Henry V's victorious army at the Battle of Agincourt (1415). The family coat of arms, proudly displayed on that occasion, can be seen today outside the hotel in Stonor village. Continued loyalty to Rome at the Reformation led to heavy fines, imprisonment and confiscation of land. During those times, Stonor House remained a centre of Catholic faith and became a hiding place for Jesuit priest Edmund Campion. He set up a secret printing press here to produce tracts attacking the new religion, an activity which led to his arrest and execution. Not until the Catholic Emancipation Act of 1829 did the family's fortunes improve.

A house has existed in Stonor Park since before the Norman Conquest. The earliest part of the present building, with its Georgian façade, dates from the 13th century; an adjacent chapel of similar age is one of only three in England to have celebrated the Catholic Mass continuously since those times (**Appendix C** gives opening times).

WALK 35

Checkendon - Stoke Row

(4¼ miles)

An easy walk between two delightful villages on the Chiltern plateau. Shaded by trees for two-thirds of the way, the route becomes a bluebell wonderland in late spring. Checkendon with its beautiful church and ancient buildings is our starting point; but the focal point is undoubtedly the Maharajah's Well at Stoke Row - a most unexpected sight in an English village.

O.S. Maps:	Landranger 175. Pathfinder 1156.
Start (663,830):	Park and start at Checkendon church. 5 miles SE of Wallingford on a minor road off the A4074.
Terrain:	Mostly level; a few gentle inclines. Five stiles.
Refreshments:	Checkendon: The Four Horseshoes (Brakspear) 01491-680325 SDA, G/PA (part of G is covered), CA, DA in G. S.
Public Transport:	From Reading: 1(C), M-Sat.

Route:

1.   For the first 100 yards you can either walk down the splendid, yew-lined drive into Checkendon Court and turn right at the end of the churchyard, or reach the same spot by going directly through the churchyard itself. Whichever route is chosen, a visit to CHECKENDON church can be recommended. The walk continues on a path beside an iron fence which veers right and left as it follows

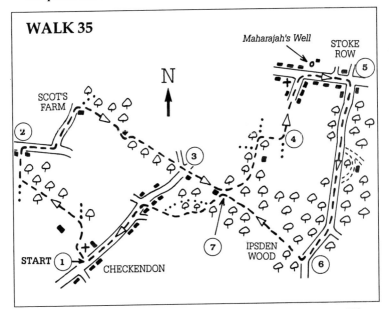

the boundary of Checkendon Court. In 200 yards, the red-brick mansion can be seen through iron gates on your left. Maintain course and soon enter a wood. After 200 yards, swing right at the edge of the trees. Proceed to the end of the wood and negotiate a stile. Keep going in the same direction across a small field to reach a metalled road. Turn right.

2.   In 200 yards our route branches left onto a road signposted to Ipsden; in a further 200 yards it comes to Scot's Farm. Immediately beyond the final barn, turn right along a well-used farm track running between woods on the left and a hedge on your right. Ignore all paths going into the woods. One hundred yards beyond a pink, wood-framed house, climb over a stile. Do not go through either of the two iron gates ahead, but follow the track as it curves left into a field. Bear right here and take a track along the right-hand field edge, beside a wood. The path eventually exits the field via a stile to enter a road junction.

3.   Cross the main road (Uxmore Road) and go down the narrow lane opposite, passing a farm on your right. In 200 yards reach a substantial brick house. Continue ahead towards Ipsden Wood. Do not enter the wood immediately but turn left, cross a small plank bridge, and take a track climbing into the trees. When the path divides, take the left fork beside a fence. As the trees come to an end on your right, pass a paddock, house and sheds before entering a small wood. In 5 yards come to a T-junction of paths. Turn right. Follow a wire fence to the edge of the wood. Proceed along a fenced track next to the trees and swing right onto a similar path between fields.

4.   At a T-junction, bear left along a farm track leading to STOKE ROW. The track soon becomes a metalled road lined with houses. Pass a flint church with an octagonal tower and turn right into a main road. In 100 yards arrive at the Maharajah's Well. After viewing the ornate structure you may wish to rest or picnic in Cherry Orchard Park before continuing along the main road.

5.   Immediately before the Cherry Tree pub, branch right into Busgrove Lane - a quiet, wooded road where you can walk on the grass verge or in the woodland. The lane gently descends through Busgrove and Basset Woods and along Splashall Bottom. In $^3/_4$ mile,

Stoke Row: the Maharajah's Well

where the road veers half left, turn sharply right onto a wide, woodland track. A Forestry Commission notice "Chiltern Forest District IPSDEN WOOD" marks the spot.

6. Known as Judge's Ride, this track may once have been used by local judges as they rode between courts. After ½ mile the wood comes to an end at a house passed on the outward journey.

7. Do not go ahead here but remain within the trees. Turn left onto an uphill path which curves right alongside a fence. Thirty yards after the track veers away from the fence you arrive at a small clearing. The main path turns right here, but the right of way proceeds ahead through holly bushes to a stile at the edge of the wood. Beyond the stile follow a right-hand field edge. After 40 yards, climb a fence and go diagonally across the next field. In the distant corner, turn right into the trees to reach a stile. (To avoid horses in the fields, you may wish to use the main path from the clearing which soon comes to a two-bar fence at the wood perimeter. Beyond the fence it goes forward through trees to arrive at the same stile.) The stile leads into a hedged path, which in 200 yards reaches a main road. Turn left. Follow the road through Checkendon village back to the starting point.

177

Points of Interest

CHECKENDON St Peter and St Paul, one of Oxfordshire's superb smaller churches, is not to be missed. Built by the Normans in flint and stone and largely unaltered, it boasts a fine carved doorway and two handsome moulded arches - one leading from nave to chancel and the other into a rare domed apse. Red ochre frescos of Christ and the apostles (13th century) decorate the apse walls and dome.

Admiral Manley, who accompanied Captain Cook on his first voyage around the world, is remembered by a marble tablet above the pulpit. A south window (1962) engraved by Lawrence Whistler is a memorial to Eric Kennington, churchwarden, artist, sculptor and friend of Lawrence of Arabia whose *The Seven Pillars of Wisdom* he illustrated.

Checkendon Court, rebuilt in the Tudor style in 1920, stands on the site of an earlier monastery.

STOKE ROW Topped with an Indian-style gilded dome, the ornate head of the Maharajah's Well proves an irresistible attraction for visitors to Stoke Row. To reach water, the well-shaft descends for 368ft (112m) through Chiltern chalk - a depth equal to the height of St Paul's cathedral. The well was an endowment of the Maharajah of Benares in 1863. It arose from his friendship with Edward Reade of Ipsden, Lieutenant-Governor of the North Western Provinces (see **Walk 32**). Thirty years earlier, Edward had sunk a well in Benares to help a small community and at the same time spoken of water shortages in his native Chilterns. An adjacent well-keeper's cottage and cherry orchard were later endowments of the Maharajah. The annual sale of cherries generated funds for upkeep of the well, allowing villagers to have a free water supply. The well remained in use until superseded by piped water in 1939.

WALK 36

Henley - Greys Court
(6 miles)

A classic Chiltern walk of diverse interest. From Henley-on-Thames the route proceeds across Badgemore End golf course before plunging into the beech trees of Lambridge Wood. Quiet grassy paths then lead us onwards to historic Greys Court and the charming village of Rotherfield Greys. Our return leg follows the secluded Hernes valley back to Henley.

O.S. Maps:	Landranger 175. Pathfinder 1156.
Start (756,826):	Park and start at Hop Gardens, Henley. From the centre of Henley take an uphill road past the Town Hall. At a red-brick/stone turret, near to the summit, turn right into Hop Gardens.
Terrain:	Gentle inclines; one short, steep climb. Sixteen stiles.
Refreshments:	Henley: a wide range available. Greys Court: Tearoom for visitors, April-Sept, M, W, F, Sat afternoons. Rotherfield Greys: The Maltsters Arms (Brakspear) 01491-628400 SDA, G, CA, CM, DA in bar and G.
Public Transport:	Rail: from Reading and stations throughout the county. Buses: from Oxford, Abingdon, Thame, Reading and many other places.

Route:

1.   Friar Park, on the left of Hop Gardens, is the HENLEY home of ex-Beatle George Harrison. Walk along the gardens to the far end and turn left into Crisp Road. Bear left again at No. 71 onto a signposted path between houses. Beyond the houses our route gradually climbs through an area of trees and scrub. As you ascend look back for good views across the Thames valley to a patchwork of green fields and wooded hills in Berkshire and Buckinghamshire.

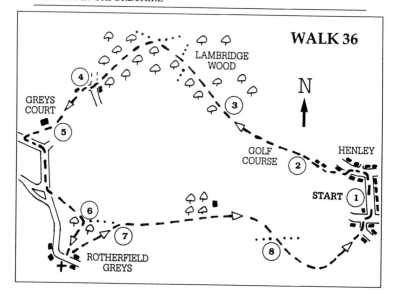

Soon pass through an iron gate and swing right into a metalled road. In 300 yards cross a stile beside a wooden gate set across the road. Continue forwards over two more stiles to join a track which follows a line of trees through Badgemore End Golf Course.

2.   Two hundred and fifty yards before reaching the far side of the golf course, this track turns left. Our route, however, maintains course alongside a row of conifers. Once beyond the mown tees, veer slightly right towards a white board at the entrance to Lambridge Wood.

3.   Yellow arrows point the way through this magnificent beech wood, carpeted by patches of bluebells in late spring. The arrows are occasionally accompanied by definitive path numbers. Our path is No. 48. When the track dips into a valley, the ancient earthworks of GRIM'S DITCH **(Walk 32)** can be seen on your left. Ignore path No. 50 which crosses the route at this point. Two hundred yards further on, near to the top of an incline, you reach a crossing of paths. Swing left here onto path No. 32. In ¹/₂ mile arrive

at a metalled road next to a cottage. Turn left. After 20 yards bear right into a lane.

4.   When the lane forks, branch left through a metal gate onto a signposted and fenced path running beside factory / farm buildings. At the final building, climb a stile on your left and immediately turn right along a field edge. The path crosses a wooden bridge next to a pond. Our route continues through a gate and uphill along the right-hand edge of the next field to reach a stile. Beyond the stile is the car park of GREYS COURT. Walk to an entrance kiosk on the far side where payment is required if you wish to enter the house or garden.

5.   In any event, bear right and proceed down the entrance drive. When the drive forks, turn right to visit the house and garden, otherwise carry on downhill. After a short distance, there are good views of Hernes valley on your left and Greys Court on the right. Follow the drive through a gate into a quiet road. Swing left and walk along the grass verge for 200 yards to reach a T-junction with a main road. Turn right. Cross to the far side and climb uphill along the verge. When the road veers right, go ahead on a minor road and in 20 yards bear left onto a signposted footpath ("Henley 2$^{1}/_{2}$"). Our route continues through trees, over a stile into a field, and along the Hernes valley. Look back from here for fine views of Greys Court. The track soon reaches Pindars Wood - a riot of colour when the bluebells are in flower.

6.   In 150 yards turn right over a stile and climb a steep path through the woods. At the far side go ahead across a field to enter ROTHERFIELD GREYS by a gate opposite the church. After exploring the village, return to the same gate and take a path along the right-hand field edge through an avenue of trees. Continue in the same direction to a gap in the field corner. In the next field, follow a path alongside a wire fence which drops down into the Hernes valley. At the valley bottom, swing right over a stile. After 150 yards climb a second stile, on your left, to reach a path running alongside a hedge. Turn right.

7.   Our route now follows this peaceful valley for 1$^{3}/_{4}$ miles back to Henley. Go over two further stiles before turning left into a farm track. The track soon crosses an open field and passes along the

Greys Court: one of the medieval towers

right-hand edge of a wood (Ash Plantation). Climb a stile beyond the wood. Note the striking, red-brick, wood-framed house of Lower Hernes on your left. Walk through more trees and negotiate another stile to enter a fenced track, which in $1/3$ mile crosses a bridleway.

8.   We now pass a sports field and car park before crossing a road to enter a tarmac path running between houses and a wood. When the path forks, continue ahead and soon enter a road. Proceed along the right-hand pavement to a T-junction. Turn left and in 200 yards arrive at a main road opposite the entrance to Friar Park and near to the starting point.

Points of Interest

HENLEY An affluent commuter town on a beautiful stretch of the Thames. Originally a Saxon settlement at a river crossing, Henley prospered during the 18th century as a coaching stop on the London to Oxford run.

Focused around its majestic bridge (1786) - whose central keystones are carved with heads of Father Thames and the goddess Isis - Henley plays host each July to the world famous Royal Regatta, as it has done ever since 1839. Before that, the very first Oxford and Cambridge boat race was rowed here in 1829.

More than 300 listed buildings grace the town's streets. Viewed from the river, two coaching inns - the Angel Inn and the Red Lion Hotel - frame the chequered tower of St Mary's church in Hart Street. Nearby are the timber-framed Chantry House (14th century) - the oldest house in Henley - and Speakers House - birthplace of William Lenthall, Speaker of the Long Parliament.

GREYS COURT Since the Norman Conquest, Greys Court has been largely in the possession of three families: the de Greys (1066-1485), the Knollyses (1518-1708) and the Stapletons (1724-1935). Robert de Grey built the original house in the 13th century. Following valiant service to Edward III at the Battle of Crecy (1346), the first Lord Grey became one of the original Knights of the Garter and was permitted to erect protective outer walls and towers.

In the 16th century the property passed to Robert Knollys, whose son, Sir Francis, rose to become Treasurer to Queen Elizabeth.

He was also in charge of Mary, Queen of Scots during her imprisonment. The Knollyses pulled down the earlier house and built the present one. Today, this Elizabethan building is surrounded by ruins of the original de Grey fortifications of which the battlemented Great Tower, three smaller towers and part of the east wall remain. In the grounds, an early Tudor building houses the largest surviving example of a donkey wheel. See **Appendix C** for opening times.

ROTHERFIELD GREYS Once part of the de Grey estate, as the name implies. The Norman church of St Nicholas, largely rebuilt in Victorian times, is the repository for some outstanding monuments to owners of Greys Court. Most spectacular is the immense, colourful tomb of Sir Francis Knollys and his wife; a figure of their son William, who built the memorial, can be seen praying on top of the canopy. William is believed to have been the inspiration for "Malvolio" in Shakespeare's *Twelfth Night*. Hidden under a carpet between the choir stalls lies one of the finest brasses in Oxfordshire - that of Robert de Grey (1387), the first Lord Grey. In 1948, the oldest tithe balance and weights in England were discovered in the church. They date from 1757 and are displayed in the Knollys chapel.

APPENDIXES

APPENDIX A: Oxfordshire: Long Distance Paths

1. The Ridgeway (89 miles) Britain's oldest road. Evidence suggests that it has been in use for some 5,000 years. The original high level track ran across chalk downs from the Bristol Channel to the Thames at Goring. In 1973 an 89-mile Ridgeway National Trail was opened between Overton Hill (Wiltshire) and Ivinghoe Beacon (Buckinghamshire). The well-signposted route runs from west to east across Oxfordshire, first along the North Wessex Downs, and then through the Chilterns. It commands extensive views of the surrounding countryside.

2. The Oxfordshire Way (65 miles) A walk across Oxfordshire from the Cotswolds to the Chilterns. Starting from Bourton-on-the-Water, just over the border in Gloucestershire, the route quietly winds its way through a rich variety of landscapes and delightful villages to Henley-on-Thames. Moderately well signposted.

3. The Thames Path (180 miles) A National Trail from the Thames Barrier to the source at Kemble in the Gloucestershire Cotswolds. Opened in 1996. The Oxfordshire section from Henley to the Gloucestershire/Wiltshire border near Lechlade totals 66 miles. Well signposted.

4. The Oxford Canal Walk (83 miles) Launched in 1995, it follows the towpath northwards from Oxford to Coventry. The canal winds its way alongside the Cherwell for 35 miles through some of the prettiest countryside in north Oxfordshire.

5. The d'Arcy Dalton Way (65 miles) Links the other four long distance paths running through the county. It is named after W.P. d'Arcy Dalton - a staunch defender of the county's fieldpaths for over fifty years. Closely following the western county boundary, the Way stretches from the Oxford Canal in the north, through ironstone hill country and the Cotswolds, to Wayland's Smithy on the Ridgeway. The route is partially signposted and sometimes obstructed.

APPENDIX B: Public Transport: Bus and Railway Companies

Buses

C	Chiltern Queens	01491-680354
CO	Charlton-on-Otmoor Coaches	01865-331249
CV	Cherwell Villager	01295-255863
G	Geoff Amos Coaches	01327-702181
GL	Grayline Coaches	01869-246461
H	Heyfordian Travel	01869-232957
J	Jeffs Coaches	01295-768292
M	Stagecoach Midland Red	01788-535555
O/CL	The Oxford Bus Co Cityline	01865-785400
P	Pulham's Coaches	01451-820369
RB	Reading Buses	01189-509509/ 594000
RR	Red Rose Travel	01296-399500
S	Swanbrook Transport	01242-574444
SD	Stagecoach Swindon & District	01793-522243
T	Thames Transit	01865-772250/ 727000
TA	Tappin's Coaches	01235-812127
TD	Thamesdown Transport	01793-523700
V	Villager Minibus Service	01451-832114
WO	Worth's Motor Services	01608-677322

Rail

GW	Great Western
TT	Thames Trains

For information about all services and fares ring:

Oxford:	01865-722333
Reading:	01734-595911
Paddington:	0345-484950 (24 hour service: calls charged at local rate)

APPENDIX C: Places to Visit

A number of historic buildings, parks and gardens mentioned in the guide are open to the public. Details of opening times and telephone numbers (where available) are given below.

Abingdon Abbey Buildings (Thames Street): M-F 2-4, Sat 10-4, Sun 12-4.

Ardington House: M afternoons in summer.

Ashdown House (National Trust): April-Oct, W, Sat 2-6. 01494-528051.

Blenheim Palace: park all year 9-4.45; palace mid-March-Oct 10.30-4.45. 01993-811325.

Brook Cottage Gardens, Alkerton: 1st April-31st Oct M-F 9-6. 01295-670303.

Broughton Castle: park all year; castle, gardens and St Mary's church 18th May-14th Sept, W, Sun, also Th in July & Aug, & Bank Hol Sun & M (inc. Easter) 2-5. 01295-262624.

Buscot Park (National Trust): house and grounds April-Sept, W-F & every 2nd & 4th weekend, 2-6; grounds only open as house but also M (but not Bank Hol M) & Tu, 2-6. 01367-242094.

Greys Court (National Trust): April-Sept. Garden M-W, F, Sat 2-6; house M, W, F 2-6. 01491-628529.

Kelmscott Manor (The Society of Antiquaries of London): April-Sept, W 11-1, 2-5. 01367-252486.

Rousham Park: gardens all year 10-4.30; house April-Sept W, Sun, Bank Hols 2-4.30. 01869-347110.

Stonor Park: April-Sept Sun, May-Sept W, July & Aug Th, Aug Sat 2-5.30; Bank Hol M 12.30-5.30. 01491-638587.

Wroxton College (Abbey): grounds open daily from dawn to dusk.

BIBLIOGRAPHY

A Guide to the Churches of Oxfordshire, J. Sherwood: Robert Dugdale 1989

Berkshire Village Book, Berkshire Federation of Women's Institutes 1972

Birds of Oxfordshire, J.W. Bruker, A.G. Gosler & A.R. Heryet: Pisces Publications 1992

Oxfordshire: A County & its People, J.G. Rhodes: Oxfordshire Museums Service 1980

Oxfordshire Parks, F. Woodward: Oxfordshire Museum Services 1982

Oxfordshire Village Book, N. Hammond: Countryside Books 1983

Philip's County Guide: Oxfordshire, ed. T. Alan 1994

Portrait of Oxfordshire, C. Bloxham: Hale 1982

Shire County Guide: Oxfordshire & Oxford, M. Yurdan 1988

The Birds of Berkshire & Oxfordshire, M.C. Radford: Longmans 1966

The Buildings of England: Berkshire, N. Pevsner: Penguin Books 1966

The Buildings of England: Oxfordshire, J. Sherwood & N. Pevsner: Penguin Books 1974

The King's England: Berkshire, A. Mee: Hodder & Stoughton 1939

The King's England: Oxfordshire, A. Mee: Hodder & Stoughton 1942 & 1965

The New Oxfordshire Village Book, Oxfordshire Federation of Women's Institutes: Countryside Books 1990

The New Shell Guides: Oxfordshire & Berkshire, R. Lethbridge: Michael Joseph Ltd 1988

The Victoria County Histories, Berkshire & Oxfordshire volumes

Upper Thames Valley Today, H. Knights: Harry Knights 1985

Walking in the Chilterns, D. Unsworth: Cicerone Press 1993

CICERONE GUIDES
Cicerone publish a wide range of reliable guides to walking and climbing in Britain, and other general interest books.

LAKE DISTRICT - General Books
CONISTON COPPER A History
CHRONICLES OF MILNTHORPE
A DREAM OF EDEN -LAKELAND DALES
EDEN TAPESTRY
THE HIGH FELLS OF LAKELAND
KENDAL A SOCIAL HISTORY
LAKELAND - A taste to remember (Recipes)
LAKELAND VILLAGES
LAKELAND TOWNS
LAKELAND PANORAMAS
THE LAKERS
THE LOST RESORT? (Morecambe)
LOST LANCASHIRE (Furness area)
REFLECTIONS ON THE LAKES
AN ILLUSTRATED COMPANION INTO LAKELAND

LAKE DISTRICT - Guide Books
THE BORDERS OF LAKELAND
BIRDS OF MORECAMBE BAY
CASTLES IN CUMBRIA
CONISTON COPPER MINES Field Guide
THE CUMBRIA CYCLE WAY
THE EDEN WAY
IN SEARCH OF WESTMORLAND
SHORT WALKS IN LAKELAND-1: SOUTH LAKELAND
SHORT WALKS IN LAKELAND- 2:NORTH LAKELAND
SCRAMBLES IN THE LAKE DISTRICT
MORE SCRAMBLES IN THE LAKE DISTRICT
THE TARNS OF LAKELAND VOL 1 - WEST
THE TARNS OF LAKELAND VOL 2 - EAST
WALKING ROUND THE LAKES
WALKS IN SILVERDALE/ARNSIDE
WESTMORLAND HERITAGE WALK
WINTER CLIMBS IN THE LAKE DISTRICT

NORTHERN ENGLAND (outside the Lakes
BIRDWATCHING ON MERSEYSIDE
CANAL WALKS Vol 1 North
CANOEISTS GUIDE TO THE NORTH EAST
THE CLEVELAND WAY & MISSING LINK
THE DALES WAY
DOUGLAS VALLEY WAY

WALKING IN THE FOREST OF BOWLAND
HADRIANS WALL Vol 1 The Wall Walk
HADRIANS WALL VOL 2 Walks around the Wall
HERITAGE TRAILS IN NW ENGLAND
THE ISLE OF MAN COASTAL PATH
IVORY TOWERS & DRESSED STONES (Follies)
THE LANCASTER CANAL
LANCASTER CANAL WALKS
A WALKERS GUIDE TO THE LANCASTER CANAL
WALKS FROM THE LEEDS-LIVERPOOL CANAL
LAUGHS ALONG THE PENNINE WAY
A NORTHERN COAST-TO-COAST
NORTH YORK MOORS Walks
ON THE RUFFSTUFF 84 Bike rides in Northern England
THE REIVERS WAY (Northumberland)
THE RIBBLE WAY
ROCK CLIMBS LANCASHIRE & NW
THE TEESDALE WAY
WALKING IN COUNTY DURHAM
WALKING IN LANCASHIRE
WALKING DOWN THE LUNE
WALKING IN THE SOUTH PENNINES
WALKING IN THE NORTH PENNINES
WALKING IN THE WOLDS
WALKS IN THE YORKSHIRE DALES (3 VOL)
WALKS IN LANCASHIRE WITCH COUNTRY
WALKS IN THE NORTH YORK MOORS (2 VOL)
WALKS TO YORKSHIRE WATERFALLS (2 vol)
WATERFALL WALKS -TEESDALE & THE HIGH PENNINES
WALKS ON THE WEST PENNINE MOORS
WALKING NORTHERN RAILWAYS (2 vol)
THE YORKSHIRE DALES A walker's guide

DERBYSHIRE PEAK DISTRICT & EAST MIDLANDS
KINDER LOG
HIGH PEAK WALKS
WHITE PEAK WAY
WHITE PEAK WALKS - 2 Vols
WEEKEND WALKS IN THE PEAK DISTRICT
THE VIKING WAY
THE DEVIL'S MILL / WHISTLING CLOUGH (Novels)

Other guides are constantly being added to the Cicerone List.
Available from bookshops, outdoor equipment shops or direct (send s.a.e. for price list) from
CICERONE, 2 POLICE SQUARE, MILNTHORPE, CUMBRIA, LA7 7PY

CICERONE GUIDES
Cicerone publish a wide range of reliable guides to walking and climbing in Britain, and other general interest books.

WALES, WELSH BORDER & WEST MIDLANDS
ASCENT OF SNOWDON
THE BRECON BEACONS
WALKING IN CHESHIRE
THE CHESHIRE CYCLE WAY
CLWYD ROCK
HEREFORD & THE WYE VALLEY A Walker's Guide
HILLWALKING IN SNOWDONIA
HILL WALKING IN WALES (2 Vols)
THE LLEYN PENINSULA COASTAL PATH
THE MOUNTAINS OF ENGLAND & WALES Vol 1 WALES
WALKING OFFA'S DYKE PATH
THE RIDGES OF SNOWDONIA
ROCK CLIMBS IN WEST MIDLANDS
SARN HELEN Walking Roman Road
SCRAMBLES IN SNOWDONIA
SEVERN WALKS
THE SHROPSHIRE HILLS A Walker's Guide
SNOWDONIA WHITE WATER SEA & SURF
WALKING DOWN THE WYE
A WELSH COAST TO COAST WALK
WELSH WINTER CLIMBS

SOUTH & SOUTH WEST ENGLAND
WALKING IN CORNWALL
WALKING IN THE CHILTERNS
COTSWOLD WAY
COTSWOLD WALKS (3 VOLS)
WALKING ON DARTMOOR
WALKERS GUIDE TO DARTMOOR PUBS
WALKING IN DEVON
WALKING IN DORSET
EXMOOR & THE QUANTOCKS
THE GRAND UNION CANAL WALK
THE KENNET & AVON WALK
LONDON THEME WALKS
WALKING IN OXFORDSHIRE
AN OXBRIDGE WALK
A SOUTHERN COUNTIES BIKE GUIDE
THE SOUTHERN-COAST-TO-COAST

SOUTH DOWNS WAY & DOWNS LINK
SOUTH WEST WAY - 2 Vol
THE TWO MOORS WAY Dartmoor-Exmoor
WALKS IN KENT Bk 2
THE WEALDWAY & VANGUARD WAY

SCOTLAND
THE BORDER COUNTRY - WALKERS GUIDE
BORDER PUBS & INNS A Walker's Guide
CAIRNGORMS WINTER CLIMBS
WALKING THE GALLOWAY HILLS
THE ISLAND OF RHUM
THE ISLE OF SKYE - A Walker's Guide
THE SCOTTISH GLENS (Mountainbike Guide)
  Book 1: THE CAIRNGORM GLENS
  Book 2 THE ATHOLL GLENS
  Book 3 THE GLENS OF RANNOCH
  Book 4 THE GLENS OF TROSSACH
  Book 5 THE GLENS OF ARGYLL
  Book 6 THE GREAT GLEN
SCOTTISH RAILWAY WALKS
SCRAMBLES IN LOCHABER
SCRAMBLES IN SKYE
SKI TOURING IN SCOTLAND
TORRIDON A Walker's Guide
WALKS from the WEST HIGHLAND RAILWAY
WINTER CLIMBS BEN NEVIS & GLENCOE

REGIONAL BOOKS UK & IRELAND
THE ALTERNATIVE PENNINE WAY
THE ALTERNATIVE COAST TO COAST
LANDS END TO JOHN O'GROATS CYCLE GUIDE
CANAL WALKS Vol.1: North
CANAL WALKS Vol.2: Midlands
CANAL WALKS Vol.3: South
LIMESTONE - 100 BEST CLIMBS
THE PACKHORSE BRIDGES OF ENGLAND
THE RELATIVE HILLS OF BRITAIN
THE MOUNTAINS OF ENGLAND & WALES
  VOL 1 WALES, VOL 2 ENGLAND
THE MOUNTAINS OF IRELAND
THE IRISH COAST TO COAST WALK

Also a full range of EUROPEAN and OVERSEAS guidebooks - walking, long distance trails, scrambling, ice-climbing, rock climbing.

Other guides are constantly being added to the Cicerone List.
Available from bookshops, outdoor equipment shops or direct (send s.a.e. for price list) from
CICERONE, 2 POLICE SQUARE, MILNTHORPE, CUMBRIA, LA7 7PY

IF YOU LIKE ADVENTUROUS ACTIVITIES ON
MOUNTAINS OR HILLS
YOU WILL ENJOY

Climber

MOUNTAINEERING / HILLWALKING /
TREKKING / ROCK CLIMBING /
SCRAMBLING IN BRITAIN AND ABROAD

AVAILABLE FROM NEWSAGENTS,
OUTDOOR EQUIPMENT SHOPS,
OR BY SUBSCRIPTION
(6-12 MONTHS) from

CALEDONIAN MAGAZINES LTD,
PLAZA TOWER, EAST KILBRIDE, GLASGOW G74 1LW
Tel: (01355) 246444 Fax: (01355) 263013

THE WALKERS' MAGAZINE

THE GREAT OUTDOORS

COMPULSIVE MONTHLY READING FOR
ANYONE INTERESTED IN WALKING

AVAILABLE FROM NEWSAGENTS,
OUTDOOR EQUIPMENT SHOPS, OR BY SUBSCRIPTION
(6-12 MONTHS) from
CALEDONIAN MAGAZINES LTD,
PLAZA TOWER, EAST KILBRIDE, GLASGOW G74 1LW
Tel: (01355) 246444 Fax: (01355) 263013

mountain sports incorporating 'Mountain INFO'

Britain's liveliest and most authorative magazine for mountaineers, climbers and ambitious hillwalkers. Gives news and commentary from the UK and worldwide, backed up by exciting features and superb colour photography.

OFFICIAL MAGAZINE

Have you read it yet?

Available monthly from your newsagent or specialist gear shop.

Call 01533 460722 for details

BRITISH MOUNTAINEERING COUNCIL